big little recipes

FOOD52

big little recipes

good food with minimal ingredients and maximal flavor

Emma Laperruque

Photographs by James Ransom
Illustrations by Hyesu Lee

TEN SPEED PRESS
California | New York

contents

salads with or without lettuce

radicchio with feta, pistachios
& salted honey 14

steak caesar with two-for-one dressing 17

all the cauliflower with grapes,
gouda & pecans 18

orange-avocado salad
with fish sauce & almonds 21

butter lettuce with sunflower-garlic
dressing & pumpernickel croutons 22

juicy cantaloupe with salami,
pepperoncini & olives 25

shaved fennel with fig
vinaigrette & blue cheese 26

blt, but make it a salad 29

smash-fried potato salad with
sweet pickles & red onion 30

raw butternut squash with
goat cheese, dates & chiles 33

if you can make cereal, you
can make salad dressing 34

bowls to dive into

bean chili 38

creamiest tomato soup without
any cream 41

french onion soup, but with leeks 42

charred carrot soup with miso 45

stop taking stock so seriously 46

cream of mushroom soup with just
cream & mushrooms 48

garlicky escarole toast in
parmesan broth 51

spicy corn soup with shiitakes
& green onions 52

brothy white beans with broccoli
rabe & pepperoni 55

chicken noodle soup with lots of dill 56

pastas, grains & bready things

meats & fishes

vegetables that aren't sides

sweet stuff to start or end the day

foreword

There are no new recipes, just new perspectives. And perspective is the personal element that makes all cooking interesting, memorable, and most of all delicious.

Emma Laperruque comes with a whole lotta perspective. She marched into our office in 2018 on a mission to write great recipes and articles. We mostly just cleared out of her way and waited for her recipes to post so we could make them ourselves.

She's our favorite kind of cook: imaginative, resourceful, intolerant of boring food. When she brought this concept to life at Food52—understanding innately that what most people want is Big. Little. Recipes.—we knew it would be a hit right off the bat. Who doesn't want to whip up a chicken dish with nothing but sesame seeds, a jar of artichoke hearts, and arugula? We're in! Or cream of mushroom soup with just cream and mushrooms? More please!

Emma delivered much more. In this, her first book (with surely many to follow), you'll find sixty recipes with minimal ingredients and maximal pleasure. There's an origami quality to Emma's work. From just rib-eyes and parsley, she shapes a complex and satisfying dinner with a built-in salad. From limes and saltines, she creates a tangy custard capped with a salty crumble.

She demands a lot from her ingredients and has the discipline of a great editor to leave all but the most essential elements out of her recipes. If super-flavorful corn stock can be made with simply corn cobs and water, why crowd it with anything else? This makes cooking her food like little adventures because you know there will be tricks and inventive twists along the way.

We hope you, too, will dive in and cook with Emma and experience the brilliant perspective she brings to the table.

Warmly,

Amanda Hesser and Merrill Stubbs
Cofounders of Food52

introduction

A dish doesn't need to have a lot of ingredients to have a lot of flavor. Or, such was my hunch when I started Big Little Recipes as a weekly column on Food52 in 2018—that something like three-ingredient oatmeal cookies or two-ingredient pasta sauce or one-ingredient chicken stock isn't delicious in spite of its minimalism but, rather, because of it.

If you don't believe me, just ask a peanut butter and jelly sandwich. According to the internet, you can supposedly upgrade this with bananas, flax seeds, marshmallow fluff, bacon, hot sauce, and, honestly, we could be here all day. But if you've ever had a PB&J, you know none of this is necessary. As one of my favorite cookbook authors Marcella Hazan used to tell her students, "What you leave out is just as important as what you put in."

And the recipes in this book leave out plenty. Besides a few pantry staples like salt and pepper, I'll never ask you to buy more than five things for a dish. This is a matter of convenience, of course, but it's also a celebration (a shindig! a rager!) of ingredients. With smart techniques—and a few wily tricks for good measure—ingredients can accomplish a lot more than we give them credit for.

Why throw out the water your beans were cooked in when it actually tastes really good? Why overcrowd a salad with seven fruits when you could spotlight just one? Why include flour in brownies in the first place? You'll find these answers and then some as you cook and bake through this collection. And along the way, I hope you start to ask your own questions whenever you grocery shop or start dinner. Minimalist cooking is all about healthy skepticism. Do I really need four different herbs as a garnish? Probably not. If I'm out of vegetable stock, will water do the job just as well? You bet.

Because these recipes are so pared-down, each ingredient stands out, so make it count. If you're able, take advantage of a local farmers' market, butcher shop, bread baker, cheese maker, grain miller, what-have-you. From a larger perspective, communities are happier with small businesses like these around. And from a selfish one, peak-summer melon just tastes better, like steak from a cow that lived a sunny, grassy life.

If you've followed along from the start (oh hi, hello, I love you), you'll probably recognize some favorites from the column that we couldn't not include. Like a Caesar dressing that doubles as a marinade, breaded chicken cutlets with no bread crumbs in sight, pasta with a two-ingredient green sauce, and buttery scones that are somehow butterless.

That said, the majority of these recipes are brand-new. The chapters aren't broken down by meal categories—because who am I to say if bacon and eggs spaghetti is breakfast or dinner? Instead, I focused on the dishes I crave most often: Fresh as heck salads. Brothy-slurpy situations. Pastas, grains, and friends. Brawny meats and briny fishes. Vegetables that don't want you to call them "sides." (Don't do it.) And sweet somethings for whenever you dang well please.

You'll also find lots of good-to-know tips, mini-recipe spreads, and choose-your-own-adventure charts. Think: a riled-up case for simpler stock, a romantic ode to canned tuna, a very good reason to always have bananas in your freezer, and more where that came from.

Obviously, I hope this book leads you toward so many good meals. But even more than that, I hope it leads you toward a feeling (yes, I know, a *feeling*) that I first remember from some summer in the mid-'90s: I'm standing in a kitchen, shorter than the countertops, ocean-soaked, bare feet. The windows are open, and my mom is next to me, smearing mayonnaise on toast, piling it with salty, juicy, Jersey tomatoes. And then she leans down and feeds me a bite.

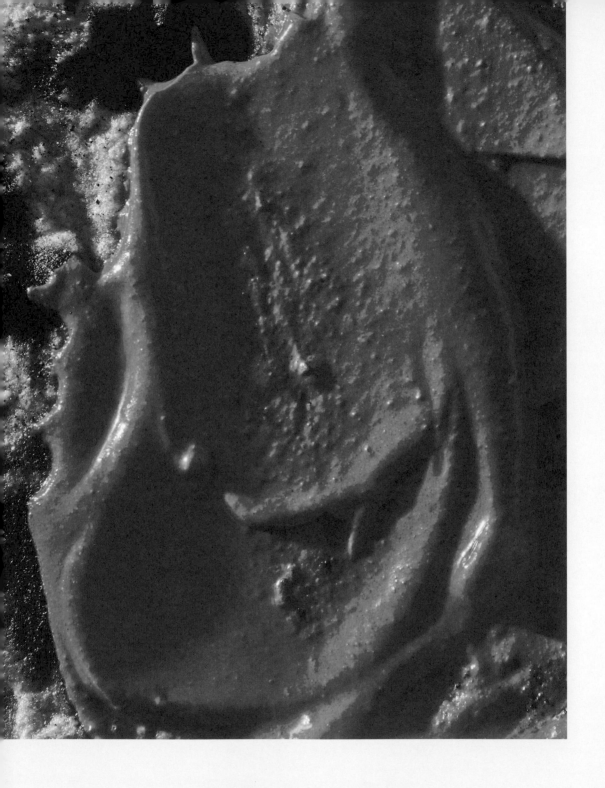

big little 101

A Big Little Recipe has the smallest ingredient list possible—but never at the expense of flavor—all thanks to these simple strategies.

Let the ingredient do its job. When you go to the barber shop, one person cuts your hair; right? Add in another stylist, and the haircut would take longer and look worse. Ingredients are the same way. If a salad—say, the cantaloupe one on page 25—has crispy salami for savoriness and crunch, there's no point in throwing in bacon, too. It would undermine what's already accomplished and overcrowd the dish along the way.

Wring each ingredient for all it's worth. Ingredients are hard-working creatures—even workaholics. So let's get the most out of them. Think about tomatoes in the summery pasta on page 83: Some get blitzed with butter, becoming a no-cook sauce, while others get sautéed into a jammy topping. Likewise, because the brownies on page 154 already include walnut hunks, a DIY walnut flour replaces the usual all-purpose.

Lean on two-for-one-ers. This could mean whole foods like beets and radishes, which come with, you know, the beets and radishes, but *also* the beet and radish greens. Or it could be ready-to-rumble products like bread-and-butter pickles and feta, which are jarred with their own flavorful brine.

Blow an ingredient out of the water. I'm usually an everything-in-moderation sort of gal—but sometimes, excess comes in handy. Take, for instance, Braised Brisket with Forty Cloves of Garlic (page 88). Would a few cloves be more reasonable? Sure. Does forty cloves yield a more savory, more memorable, more repeat-worthy brisket? Definitely. The same goes for the amount of dill in chicken soup (page 56), which seems outrageous, but is actually just-right.

Replace one ingredient with another. In the simplest recipes, no substitute goes unnoticed. This means you get to keep the same little ingredient list and end up with a brand-new, better-than-ever dish. Case in point: the apple turnovers on page 134, where a classic pie pastry ditches butter and calls in cheddar—yes, cheddar—instead.

Use the same ingredients but a different technique. The cheffy term for this is *deconstructed*, but I prefer *shaking things up*. If there's a few-ingredient recipe you love, odds are it can be reborn as something just as lovable. Start with the elements of a BLT sandwich, take a few detours, and you can easily end up with a salad (hi, bacon fat–fried croutons; hello, tomato-mayo dressing). Likewise, looking at an ingredient from a fresh perspective, like the raw butternut squash on page 33, can make an otherwise simple dish stand out.

must-haves

Every recipe in this book has five ingredients or fewer—not counting the following pantry staples (dare I say, superstars?), which are so hardworking that my kitchen is never without them.

black pepper

Always freshly ground, but maybe not how you'd expect. Between us, I don't like pepper mills for cooking (though one on the table is nice). I like measuring by the spoonful and sprinkling oversize pinches, neither of which a hand-crank is good at. Just pulse black peppercorns in a coffee grinder (or, if you have more patience than I do, a mortar and pestle) and transfer to a tiny, lidded jar, where they can stay feisty for several days until you're ready for another round.

butter

A hunk of salted, cultured butter lives alongside my toaster for, well, toast—and off-the-cuff pantry pasta, boiled potatoes, etc. But unless otherwise stated, unsalted American-style butter is the default. It allows you to adjust seasoning to taste, the most exciting step of any recipe. Swapping in European-style butter won't make much of a difference in savory recipes, but proceed with caution when it comes to baked goods, which are sensitive to substitutes.

extra-virgin olive oil

It's handy to keep two types of olive oil in stock. The first is what I think of as all-purpose—easily within budget and preferably purchased in bulk. I buy 3-quart tins (better price, less waste) to fill a cruet on my counter. The second is what Ina Garten would call "good"—as fancy as you can swing, for plunking the final exclamation point on a dish. Drizzle on a crisp salad, a boiled vegetable, a charred steak.

neutral oil

Low in flavor, high in smoke point, a neutral oil can go in a lot of directions: Vegetable and canola are accessible and interchangeable, but grapeseed or peanut can often accomplish the same job if that's what you happen to have around. Like all-purpose olive oil, I buy this in the biggest container I can get my hands on, then transfer it to a smaller bottle that lives on my counter.

salt

There are two varieties of salt in my kitchen, each in a speckled cellar big enough to reach into and grab by the handful: The first is Diamond Crystal kosher salt (to convert to Morton's, halve the called-for quantity, then adjust to taste). When I say to "generously" season boiling water with salt, be it for pasta or vegetables, eyeball 1 teaspoon to 1 tablespoon Diamond Crystal per 1 quart water. The second is flaky salt, like Maldon or Jacobsen, for crunching between your fingertips and sprinkling on everything from salad to cookies.

water!

Yes, water is tasteless compared to something like wine or stock, but that doesn't mean it's second place. Next to salt, this is the MVI (most valuable ingredient) in a Big Little pantry—more details on page 10.

good-to-haves

If you see these ingredients, consider them part of the tally. That said, you're going to see them a fair amount. Each one is multipurpose as heck, like shampoo that's also face wash that's also dish soap that's also laundry detergent.

anchovies

Rinsing and filleting salt-packed anchovies was one of my prep tasks as a baker. But unlike slicing green onions (page 10), this one taught me to run the other way: Oil-packed anchovies are too convenient to pass up. And unless you're eating them straight (which I respect), it's hard to tell the difference. Mash a fillet or two into oil and vinegar for an upgraded vinaigrette. Or mayo for a fuss-free crudités dip. Or soft butter for happier toast, pasta (page 65), or grains (rice, kasha, wheat berries, you name it). Or tomato sauce. Or cream for braising vegetables (page 113).

bread

There's never not sliced bread in my freezer—mostly for half-asleep toast, but also salad croutons, minimalist veggie burgers (page 122), hangry grilled cheese (page 70), and extra-saucy dinners. Don't forget to freeze those loaf butts for crumbs (see the how-to on page 120). If you haven't already, find a local bakery to call your own, somewhere you can swing by most weekends to snag a warm loaf (and a coffee for the road).

cultured dairy

Greek yogurt, sour cream, crème fraîche, buttermilk: These multitalented ingredients serve up richness *and* tanginess, which is extra handy when it comes to quickie sauces (just blitz with a tender herb as on page 95) and on-a-whim salad dressings (lots of two-ingredient options on page 34). Psst: Yes, 2 percent yogurt is great with granola, but whole-milk yogurt is best for cooking—its flavor is like a bear hug, whereas low-fat alternatives are like a handshake.

green onions

Another one of my prep tasks, this time as a line cook, was slicing green onions—on a bias, thin as possible, every shift. Somewhere along the way, I became enamored with this ingredient—as much allium as herb as hearty green. After using the green part, stick the white roots (figure 1 to 2 inches' worth) in a tiny jar of water, like flowers. Set somewhere sunny and the onions will start regrowing in a matter of days.

mayonnaise

Store-bought mayo has never steered me wrong, especially when mixed with another ingredient like grape tomatoes (page 29), pickle brine (page 34), or canned tuna (page 99). Worth noting: Mayo, not butter, is the superior spread for grilled cheese (page 70). Also: Try smearing proteins, like pounded chicken breasts or pork chops, with mayo, then dredge in bread crumbs and pan-fry.

pickled or fermented anything

Bread-and-butter pickles, sauerkraut, kimchi, capers . . . these briny-funky ingredients are as long-lasting as they are flavorful. Whether it's quick-pickled or lacto-fermented, you've got an assertively flavored cucumber chip, cabbage wedge, etc.—and a just-as-confident brine to use instead of vinegar.

water up

Water down is another way of saying dilute value. Which is—how do I put this?—baloney. Water is one of the most cost-effective, dynamic, powerful ingredients. Think of it this way: Water plus something-else equals . . .

Any stock. Whether you're simmering beans or blanching greens, water is often seen as a means to an end, not the end in itself. But why, when water soaks up flavor like a sponge? Enter: Eight tiny stock recipes on page 46.

Not-from-a-cow milk. Blend water with raw nuts, and you earn a creamy nondairy milk to put toward a herd (sorry, couldn't help it) of dishes. Same goes for other dry goods, such as rolled oats and coconut flakes.

Makeshift vegetable soup. Pureed vegetables plus water equals soup? Yep. So long as you season liberally (start with the miso template on page 45), this is a surefire strategy for whatever's about to take a turn for the worse in the crisper.

Silkier pasta sauce. The starchy-salty water in which your pasta cooks is as valuable as the pasta itself. Either remove the noodles with a spider or tongs— or reserve a mug-full of the water before draining the pasta into a colander. This liquid can enrich eggs a la carbonara (page 61) or stretch pureed vegetables.

Never-dry meatballs or meatloaf. A splashy trick I learned from Rao's Genius meatballs: Any ground-meat situation loves a tall drink of water. Think of it like moisture insurance—even if you forget the meatloaf (page 96) in the oven after the timer goes off.

Better veggie burgers. Combine dried chickpeas with water before you head to bed, and you're halfway to falafel-esque, never-mushy veggie burgers (three variations on page 122). Save the canned beans for something else, like the low-and-slow fish on page 102.

Crisper salads. Jumping into cold water isn't fun for humans, but, boy, do vegetables love it. Whether it's limp romaine or wilting celery, a quick dunk in an icy bath yields a refreshed crunch. What's more: With bitter chicories like radicchio (page 14), the water wards off bitterness.

Creamy dressings. Whether it's tahini or sunflower butter (page 22), whatever nut or seed paste is in your kitchen would love to turn into dressing. When this fatty ingredient combines with water, it essentially acts as oil, emulsifying into something pourable, creamy, and lush.

salads with or without lettuce

radicchio with feta, pistachios & salted honey

The biggest problem with my husband is that he hates radicchio. We both agree it's bitter, only he means this as a critique, while I say it as a compliment. Luckily, there are many ways to mellow chicories. You can add something salty or fatty or sweet, or plunge the leaves into ice water. This salad—with broken-up feta, crunchy pistachios, and a sticky honey dressing—check-check-checks all those boxes. But the best part is what happens beforehand: Instead of water, the radicchio swan-dives into feta brine, a bonus ingredient you'll have around anyway. As the liquid draws out sharpness, the leaves become livelier, saltier, snappier, cheesier. This dish would be happy to hang out with any protein, like roast chicken, grilled fish, or braised beans.

SERVES 2 TO 4

2 small heads radicchio

4 ounces (115g) feta, crumbled, brine reserved

½ cup (70g) shelled raw pistachios, roughly chopped

Extra-virgin olive oil

Honey

¼ teaspoon kosher salt

Halve the radicchio heads, remove and discard the cores, then roughly chop. Combine 1 to 1½ cups feta brine (depending on how much is in the container), 1½ cups cold water, and 2 cups ice cubes in a large bowl. Stir until the brine is super cold, then strain out the ice cubes. Add the radicchio, toss to coat, and weigh down with a small plate to submerge. Soak for about 15 minutes, stirring every so often. By the end, the radicchio should be slightly feta-y and noticeably less bitter.

While that's going, add the pistachios to a skillet (I like cast-iron here) and set over medium-low heat. Toast, shaking every so often and lowering the heat if they're browning too quickly, until the nuts are very fragrant, 8 to 12 minutes. Keep a watchful eye since burnt nuts are bad nuts. Pour onto a plate to cool.

Add 2 tablespoons oil, 2 tablespoons honey, and the salt to a tiny bowl and stir with a fork until mostly combined.

When the radicchio is ready to get out of its bath, use tongs to transfer it to a salad spinner and dry well. (If it's wet, the dressing will have trouble grabbing hold.)

Dump the dried radicchio into a bowl, pour the honey dressing on top, and toss until evenly coated. Transfer to a platter or individual plates, then top with the crumbled feta and toasted pistachios. Finish with a squiggle each of oil and honey.

steak caesar with two-for-one dressing

If you want to get technical about it, dressing is a ready-to-wear sauce that coats things, like raw lettuce or roasted vegetables. Marinade is a salty-tangy hangout where meat, fish, or vegetables take it easy for a while, becoming more flavorful and juicy, often before being cooked. In this recipe though? They're the exact same thing. The inspiration was Caesar dressing, only without the Worcestershire, garlic, Dijon, and egg yolks, all of which I admire but don't always need. The other ingredients—Parmesan, anchovies, lemon, olive oil, and black pepper—can more than hold their own. Some of this marinade-dressing (marinessing? darinade?) goes toward flank steak, a big-flavor, tough-attitude cut in need of some tenderizing. The rest gets tossed with crunchy romaine. This is a generous dinner for two. If you throw some warm bread or potatoes alongside, you can stretch that to three or four.

Add the Parmesan to the bowl of a food processor and pulse until it's finely ground. Take out 2 tablespoons and save for later. Add the anchovies to the food processor and pulse until minced. Add the lemon juice, ½ teaspoon pepper, and 6 tablespoons of the oil and process until smooth and thick like mayo, scraping down the sides as needed.

Season the steak lightly with salt and pepper, then put it in an airtight container along with a scant ⅓ cup of the dressing (refrigerate the rest for the salad), making sure the meat is fully covered. Refrigerate the steak for 4 to 12 hours.

When you're ready to eat, heat a cast-iron skillet over medium-high heat. Use an offset spatula or butter knife to scrape off as much marinade as possible from the steak (this helps it brown better). Add the remaining 1 tablespoon oil to the hot pan, then add the steak. Cook it for about 5 minutes per side for medium-rare (130°F to 135°F/55°C to 57°C).

Let the steak rest on a cutting board while you toss the romaine and remaining dressing in a serving bowl or platter.

Slice the steak as thinly as possible against the grain, then scatter it on top of the salad. Serve with the lemon wedges, the reserved Parmesan, and more pepper.

SERVES 2 TO 4

3 ounces (85g) Parmesan, chopped into chunks

1 (2-ounce/55g) tin oil-packed anchovy fillets, drained

¼ cup (60ml) freshly squeezed lemon juice, plus lemon wedges for serving

Freshly ground black pepper

7 tablespoons (105ml) extra-virgin olive oil

12 ounces (340g) flank steak

Kosher salt

2 romaine hearts, roughly chopped

all the cauliflower with grapes, gouda & pecans

The twenty-first century has been kind to cauliflower. While this vegetable used to be a less-cool cousin to broccoli, its popularity has gone through the roof thanks to an uncanny ability to become whatever you want: pizza crust, ground-beef taco (see page 117), bowl of rice, bag of flour, brand-new car. But to me, the wildest metamorphosis cauliflower can make is from raw to roasted. To really appreciate this crunchy-creamy contrast, just put the two next to each other in the same dish. If you don't have a mandoline, I urge (implore!) you to get one. It's a game changer for shaved-vegetable salads like this, and shaved-vegetable salads are game changers for weeknights, or whenever you're having people over and want to be all, "Oh this? It was nothing." Following in the cauliflower's footsteps, the grapes are also raw and roasted. And, for good measure, salty gouda and fatty pecans keep things from feeling too pure.

SERVES 4 TO 6

1 cup (120g)
pecan pieces

2 large heads cauliflower

7 tablespoons (105ml)
extra-virgin olive oil,
plus more to taste

Kosher salt

3 cups (480g) red grapes

2 tablespoons sherry
vinegar, plus more
to taste

4 ounces (115g)
aged gouda, diced

Turn on the oven to 450°F (230°C). Immediately dump the pecans onto a baking sheet and roast while the oven is heating, 7 to 10 minutes, until toasty and fragrant. Transfer the pecans to a plate to cool.

Remove the green leaves from both cauliflower heads and thinly slice the leaves, like celery. Add these to a big bowl.

Quarter one cauliflower head, remove its core, then chop the quarters into florets. Place the florets on a baking sheet, add 4 tablespoons of the oil and ¾ teaspoon salt, and toss. Roast for 20 to 25 minutes, stirring halfway through, until tender and deeply browned.

On the warm baking sheet used to toast the pecans, combine 1½ cups (240g) of the grapes with 1 tablespoon of the oil and a pinch of salt; shake the pan so the grapes are coated. Add the grapes to the oven when the cauliflower has about 15 minutes left and roast the grapes until soft and slouchy.

Quarter the remaining cauliflower head, remove its core, then super-thinly slice each quarter with a knife or mandoline and add to the bowl with the leaves. Chop the remaining 1½ cups (240g) grapes in half (some crosswise, some lengthwise for a mix of shapes) and add to the same bowl. Season with the remaining 2 tablespoons oil and the vinegar, plus ¾ teaspoon salt.

When the cauliflower and grapes are out of the oven, dump the raw portion of the salad onto a platter and top with the roasted grapes (and their pan juices), the roasted cauliflower, toasted pecans, and cheese. Finish with a big drizzle each of oil and vinegar.

a genius way to break down brassicas

For most of my life, I chopped cauliflower (and broccoli) into florets by starting at the frilly top. You too? But then our resident genius Kristen Miglore taught me a better way: Cut each floret, one by one, where it connects to the stalk, like you're trimming branches from a tree trunk. Will this take a little longer? Yes. Will you end up with a million less fuzzies (a term!) all over your cutting board, countertops, and floor? Yes.

not-fish sauce

If you're a vegetarian or vegan, you might, understandably, be tempted to hop over this recipe. But don't. While there's no identical substitute for fish sauce, there are salty, umami-laden standbys, perhaps already in your pantry. Try soy sauce, liquid aminos, or a combo of the two.

orange-avocado salad with fish sauce & almonds

I like bacon and eggs, or beans and rice, or chocolate and peanut butter, oranges and avocados just work. It's an opposites-attract compatibility. Oranges are splashy and tangy; avocados are buttery and rich. You could put them together, dust with salt, and impress anyone. Which reminds me, there's no added salt in this recipe. It hitches a ride from other places: the fish sauce and crunchy almonds (or any nut you fancy).

Fish sauce—known as nước mắm in Vietnam, nam pla in Thailand, and gyoshō in Japan, to name a few—is a big-personality ingredient in many Asian cuisines. Made from salted, fermented fish such as anchovies, it's invaluable anywhere you want an umami jolt. In this salad, it teams up with just-squeezed orange juice, inspired by Vietnamese nước chấm (fish sauce, water, lime juice, sugar—depending on the recipe) for a two-ingredient, no-oil-needed dressing.

If you can, opt for including different-colored oranges (say, navel and Cara Cara). And do make sure to refrigerate them beforehand—it makes the whole dish a million times more refreshing. This is just as welcome in the summer alongside grilled anything as it is in the winter when you're wanting a little sunshine.

Cut one orange in half and squeeze its juice into a glass—¼ cup (60ml) of this will go toward our dressing; the rest you can slurp up as a cook's treat. Slice off the ends of the remaining four oranges, then stand them upright on the cutting board. Use your knife to remove the peel from top to bottom, getting as much pith as possible. Slice each orange crosswise into rounds and arrange these on a platter.

Halve the avocados and discard the pits. Now halve each half and peel away the skin. Cut the avocado quarters into chunks and/or slivers. Distribute the pieces on top of the oranges.

Add the fish sauce to the ¼ cup of orange juice and stir. Taste and add more fish sauce if you'd like, then pour over the oranges and avocados.

Crush the almonds in a mortar and pestle until some are powdery, some chunky, and some whole (a cutting board and knife also works). Shower all over the salad.

SERVES 4

5 oranges, very cold

2 large ripe avocados

2 teaspoons fish sauce, plus more to taste

½ cup (70g) roasted, salted almonds

butter lettuce with sunflower-garlic dressing & pumpernickel croutons

Nuts and seeds are an easy way to add bulk and crunch to salads—just scatter a handful on top—but these ingredients can almost as easily become the salad dressing, too. This technique borrows a page from tehina (the Israeli word for "tahini") sauce, which, at its simplest, is mostly tahini and water, plus lemon juice, garlic, and salt to taste. And no, I didn't forget to mention the oil—we just don't need it. Because when you emulsify something fatty, like a nut or seed butter, with water, you end up with a dressing creamy enough to rival classic ranch that just happens to be vegan. Here, sunflower seeds do all the heavy lifting. You can buy already roasted and salted ones for ease. Or start with raw, toast them in a skillet over medium-low heat, stirring occasionally, for 10 minutes or so until golden, then season with salt. And if you can't find a pumpernickel bagel, swap in pumpernickel bread or another bagel you love.

SERVES 2

10 tablespoons (95g) roasted, salted sunflower seeds

1 large or 2 small garlic cloves, peeled

3½ tablespoons freshly squeezed lemon juice, plus more as needed

Kosher salt and freshly ground black pepper

1½ tablespoons extra-virgin olive oil

1 pumpernickel bagel, torn into bite-size pieces

1 head butter lettuce (Bibb or Boston)

Add 6 tablespoons (60g) of the sunflower seeds and the garlic to a small food processor or blender and process until the seeds turn buttery, a minute or so. Add the lemon juice and 3½ tablespoons cold water and process again until smooth, scraping down the sides as needed. Add more lemon juice, water, or both until the dressing reaches a creamy, pourable consistency. Season with salt and pepper to taste.

Set a cast-iron or nonstick skillet over medium heat and add the oil. When that's hot, add the bagel pieces, sprinkle with salt and pepper, and toss. Cook for about 4 minutes, stirring occasionally and lowering the heat as needed so they don't burn, until the bread is crispy on the outside but still squishy if you squeeze a crouton between your fingers. Cut the heat and let the croutons cool in the pan.

Lop off the bottom of the lettuce, then pull apart the leaves. Tear the big ones into bite-size pieces; leave the little ones alone. Wash, then dry well (if there's excess water on the lettuce, the dressing will slide off) and add to a big bowl.

Add the dressing to the lettuce and toss until completely coated. Divide the dressed salad between two plates, then evenly top with the croutons and the remaining 4 tablespoons (35g) sunflower seeds.

potato, potahto, tomato, tomahto... salami, salumi?

In Italian, salumi is the umbrella term for cured meats. This covers a ton of ingredients, like prosciutto, mortadella, capocollo, bresaola, and, yes, salami. That said, salami isn't one thing either—you've got pepperoni, hard, soppressata, and Genoa, to name just a few. Way back when I was a rugrat grocery shopping with my mom, she would score me a sample slice from the deli counter to keep the temper tantrums at bay. This works for adults, too.

juicy cantaloupe with salami, pepperoncini & olives

When did fruit salad become *fruit salad*? You know the one, with pineapple hunks, kiwi chunks, squished blueberries, and sad strawberries. This is a savory alternative that I like a lot better. Instead of cleaning out the produce aisle, buy just one ingredient—and make it good—say, that heavy cantaloupe that smells like honey at the stem. And instead of dressing up something sweet with more sweet, opt for meaty or salty or spicy or tangy. Or better yet, all of the above. Here, that means oven-crisped salami, pickled pepperoncini (shout-out to their brine, which turns into a stupid-easy vinaigrette), and wrinkly olives. This would be a welcome side at any backyard cookout, but I'd just as gladly call it a meal in itself.

Heat the oven to 400°F (200°C). Stack the salami and use a knife to score around the perimeter in four places (imagine 2 o'clock, 4 o'clock, 8 o'clock, and 10 o'clock); this prevents puffing in the oven. Spread the salami slices on a rimmed baking sheet and bake for 10 to 20 minutes, until crisp.

While that's in the oven, remove the cantaloupe's skin and seeds, then chop into bite-size chunks. Add these to a bowl along with the pepperoncini, ¼ cup (60ml) pepperoncini brine, and the olives. Toss, taste, and add more brine if you want.

When the salami is done, transfer the slices to a plate to cool. If there's rendered fat on the baking sheet, use a heatproof, flexible spatula to swoosh it onto the cantaloupe salad and toss to combine. Transfer the salad to a platter or individual plates, then crumble the salami on top.

SERVES 4

4 ounces (115g)
sliced Genoa salami

1 ripe, medium
cantaloupe

⅔ cup (80g) thinly
sliced pepperoncini,
brine reserved

½ cup (80g) pitted
oil-cured olives,
roughly chopped

shaved fennel with fig vinaigrette & blue cheese

Jam often finds itself in breakfasty situations, like peanut buttered toast or warm biscuits, but it wants to be part of dinner, too. Especially salad. Just remember two parts jam to one part vinegar to one part olive oil by volume, and you can whip up a tangy-sweet, highly popular vinaigrette at any time. I love fig jam (those crunchy little seeds!)—but what do you already have in the fridge? Apple, apricot, peach, or plum jam works wonders just the same. Make sure you get a wedge of creamy blue cheese and break it apart by hand; the pre-crumbled stuff is often chalky. This could be a speedy meal with some canned beans or warm bread, or a sidekick to a heartier main, like fish, chicken, or tempeh.

SERVES 4 TO 6

2 large fennel bulbs, stalks still attached

½ teaspoon kosher salt

2 tablespoons fig jam

1 tablespoon white wine vinegar

1 tablespoon extra-virgin olive oil

4 ounces (115g) blue cheese, crumbled

Pluck a handful of fennel fronds (discard the rest) and roughly chop. Cut the base of the stalks to separate them from the bulbs. With a knife or mandoline, thinly slice the stalks into coins or ribbons and add to a big bowl. Halve the bulbs lengthwise, thinly slice into half-moons, and add to the bowl. Sprinkle with the salt and toss with your hands until the fennel feels damp.

Combine the jam, vinegar, and oil in a small bowl and whisk with a fork until creamy. Dunk in a fennel piece, taste, and tweak the vinaigrette to be sweeter, sourer, richer, or whatever you want. (Just remember the cheese is sharp and funky.)

Pour the dressing on top of the fennel and toss. Taste again and adjust if needed, then transfer the fennel to a platter if you're in the mood. Top with the blue cheese and fennel fronds.

blt, but make it a salad

Instead of piling on top of each other like siblings, BLT ingredients join forces like superheroes. Bacon renders smoky-porky fat that's used to fry bread hunks into superlative croutons. Juicy tomatoes become toppers *and* morph into a two-ingredient dressing. (Sound impossible? We've got a bunch of 'em on page 34.) And lettuce, which is usually the shyest component in a BLT, now gets to show off, as it should. I opt for something ruffly and tender, like butter lettuce, though you could certainly go with iceberg, romaine, or even frisée. If you can, eat this outside in a patch of sun.

Add the bacon to a cast-iron or nonstick skillet set over medium heat. Cook for about 8 minutes, shuffling and flipping the bacon, and lowering the heat as needed so it doesn't burn, until it's as crispy as you like.

While the bacon is cooking, cut the crust off the bread slices (save these for crumbs—see page 120), then tear the slices into bite-size pieces.

When the bacon is done, transfer it to a plate—but keep the fat in the skillet and the heat on medium. Add the bread pieces to the pan, sprinkle with a pinch each of salt and pepper, then toss. Cook for about 4 minutes, stirring occasionally and lowering the heat as needed so it doesn't scorch, until the bread is browned and crispy on the outside but still squishy on the inside. Turn off the heat and let the croutons cool in the skillet.

Lop off the bottom of the lettuce head, then pull apart the leaves and tear them into bite-size pieces. Wash and dry well. (If there's excess water, the dressing will slide off.)

Add ⅔ cup (110g) of the tomatoes and the mayo to a blender or food processor. Season with salt and pepper. Process until smooth, scraping down the sides as needed. Tweak the salt and pepper to taste.

Halve the remaining tomatoes. Crumble the cooled bacon.

To assemble, combine the lettuce and half of the croutons in a big bowl. Add the tomato dressing and toss. Divide the dressed salad between plates and sprinkle the tomatoes, bacon, and remaining croutons on top.

SERVES 2 TO 4

4 thick slices bacon

2 or 3 thick slices sourdough bread

Kosher salt and freshly ground black pepper

1 head butter lettuce (Bibb or Boston)

1 pint (320g) grape or cherry tomatoes

¼ cup (60g) mayonnaise

smash-fried potato salad with sweet pickles & red onion

When I say potato salad, perhaps you picture boiled potatoes tossed with mayonnaise and set on a picnic table; then your cousin's golden retriever comes out of nowhere, steals a cheeseburger, and someone screams. This is not that. Because after being boiled, the potatoes get squashed and pan-crisped until they're halfway to French fries. (Golf ball–size spuds work best here, but if you can find only slightly smaller or larger ones, just adjust the cook times as needed.) I could eat a plate of these plain and be a happy woman. But things get even happier with the addition of crunchy bread-and-butter pickles: Scatter some on top, and mix others with mayo and a splash of sweet brine, like an unfussy tartar sauce. Then use *more* brine for red onion quick-pickles. Instead of tossing everything in a bowl, throw this on a platter and call it a day.

SERVES 4

1 medium red onion, thinly sliced into half-moons

Kosher salt

1 cup (175g) bread-and-butter pickles, plus 2 tablespoons minced, brine reserved

2 pounds (910g) small yellow potatoes

½ cup (120g) mayonnaise

Freshly ground black pepper

Neutral oil

Fill a stockpot with water and set over high heat.

Add the onion to a small bowl and season with ½ teaspoon salt. Stir until the onion starts to wilt, then pour ¼ cup (60ml) pickle brine on top.

When the water reaches a boil, generously season it with salt. Add the potatoes and cook until fork-tender, 8 to 12 minutes, checking frequently. Drain and spread out the potatoes on a baking sheet to cool for a couple minutes.

Combine the mayonnaise, minced pickles, and 1 teaspoon brine in a small bowl. Season with salt, pepper, and brine to taste.

Use a measuring cup or kitchen towel and the palm of your hand to carefully flatten each potato, aiming to keep it in one piece as much as possible. Set your largest skillet, preferably cast-iron, over medium heat and add enough oil so the potatoes will be half-submerged. When the oil is hot, add one potato—it should sizzle right away (if not, let the oil heat some more). Add enough potatoes to comfortably fill the pan. Cook for 3 to 5 minutes per side (tongs are great for flipping), until deeply golden brown and crisp. Transfer to a wire rack and sprinkle with salt and pepper. Cook the remaining potatoes in the same way, adding more oil if the skillet starts to look dry.

Once all of the potatoes are ready, swoosh the pickle mayo on a platter. Randomly scatter the potatoes, pickled onions, and bread-and-butter pickles on top.

raw butternut squash with goat cheese, dates & chiles

Yes, you can eat butternut squash raw. And you should. When left in its natural state—not roasted, not sautéed, not boiled—it tastes like the superhero alter-ego of a carrot, with a buttery flavor, snappy texture, and neon color. Though you can shave the squash into ribbons with a vegetable peeler, I prefer the slaw-like crunch of matchsticks, which take some patience, sure, but are worth it, especially if you turn on music while you chop, chop, chop. Any hot pepper works here—jalapeño, fresno, and serrano are all reliable picks. Likewise, the vinegar is flexible: If you don't have rice, try another mild variety, like apple cider or white wine. Dates can make way for jumbo raisins or tart cherries. And in lieu of fresh goat cheese, feta works wonders. Just don't cook the squash.

Combine the chile, vinegar, and a pinch of salt in a small bowl.

Peel the squash and julienne into thin-as-possible matchsticks. I do this by cutting the top of the squash into rounds, stacking those, and slicing. Then halve the bottom of the squash, scoop out the seeds, and slice. Add the matchsticks to a big bowl, season with salt to taste, and toss. Let hang out for at least 5 minutes to slightly wilt.

Meanwhile, halve, pit, and slice the dates.

Add the soaked chiles, spicy vinegar, and dates to the butternut squash. Drizzle with oil (I eyeball a few tablespoons) and toss. Taste and adjust the salt, vinegar, and oil if needed.

Transfer the salad to a platter or plates. Crumble the cheese into bite-size pieces and sprinkle these on top.

SERVES 4 TO 6

1 or 2 fresh chiles, thinly sliced

3 tablespoons rice vinegar

Kosher salt

1 medium butternut squash

6 to 8 Medjool dates

Extra-virgin olive oil

6 ounces plain goat cheese

if you can make cereal, you can make salad dressing

I'm never going to whip up ranch dressing on a weeknight. Which isn't to say I don't love ranch—I do!—but anything that asks me to take out buttermilk, mayo, sour cream, vinegar, Worcestershire, hot sauce, several fresh herbs, and multiple ground spices is going to have to wait until Saturday.

Salad dressing doesn't need more than two ingredients. And I'm not talking about oil and vinegar, the simplest template of all time. Each recipe here requires as little effort as a vinaigrette, but delivers ranch-level flavor. Just stir together with a fork, salt to taste, and put toward whatever's for dinner (each recipe yields roughly enough for two servings). Or scale up a batch and use it all week.

zingy sour cream

¼ cup (60g) sour cream

+

2 tablespoons
pepperoncini brine

+

1 tablespoon minced
pepperoncini

Dress up: grilled zucchini, crispy chicken thighs (page 87), leftover pizza

dill pickle mayo

¼ cup (60g) mayonnaise

+

2 tablespoons
dill pickle brine

+

1 tablespoon
minced dill pickle

Dress up: steak salad, cabbage slaw, blanched asparagus

buttermilk avocado

½ large ripe avocado, mashed

+

⅓ to ½ cup
(80ml to 120ml) buttermilk

**Dress up: raw radishes, salted
mango, pulled pork (page 91) tacos**

horseradish tahini

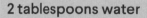

3 tablespoons tahini

+

2 tablespoons water

+

4 teaspoons prepared
horseradish

**Dress up: sautéed broccoli, roasted
butternut squash, grain bowl (page 62)**

creamy miso

¼ cup (60ml) heavy cream

+

1 scant tablespoon
red miso

**Dress up: butter lettuce, cucumber
salad, baked sweet potato**

low-lift blue cheese

2 ounces (55g) blue cheese

+

¼ cup (60g) whole-milk
yogurt or buttermilk

**Dress up: sliced tomato, shaved
celery, cold roast chicken**

bowls to dive into

bean chili

Chili recipes—even the ones without meat—are maximalists. After reading just a handful, I crossed paths with onions, carrots, peppers, garlic, dried chiles, chili powder, ground cumin, dried oregano, bay leaves, canned tomatoes, tomato juice, kidney beans, cannellini beans, black beans, chickpeas, soy sauce, masa . . .

This version whittles that list to five. In one pot on a weeknight. Chopping and browning some beans mimics ground meat, while leaving others whole adds chunky-hunky texture. Chili powder streamlines a slew of ingredients and steps, and blooming it in hot fat powers up its flavor. Onions and poblanos add savoriness and just enough kick-in-the-pants. Tomatoes bring body and broth and tang. And water encourages everyone to hold hands. That all said, I can't help myself when it comes to toppings. Grated cheese, sour cream, shredded lettuce, sliced radishes, cilantro, hot sauce? I want all of it. But everyone's a hypocrite.

SERVES 4 TO 6

2 (15.5-ounce/440g) cans kidney beans

6 tablespoons (85g) unsalted butter

Kosher salt

2½ tablespoons chili powder

1 large yellow onion, half diced, half roughly chopped

2 large poblanos, 1 diced, the other roughly chopped

1 (28-ounce/795g) can whole peeled tomatoes

Drain and rinse one can of beans and set aside. Drain, rinse, and pat-dry the beans from the other can, then dump them onto a cutting board and roughly chop.

Set a stockpot over medium heat and add 2 tablespoons of the butter. Once it's melted, add the chopped beans and spread into an even layer. Fry for about 5 minutes, until crispy, stirring once at most (the less you fuss, the better they brown). Transfer to a plate and sprinkle with salt.

Immediately add another 2 tablespoons of the butter to the pot. When melted, add the chili powder. Cook for 15 to 30 seconds, until fragrant, stirring constantly to make sure it doesn't burn. Add the onion and poblanos, 2 tablespoons water, and ½ teaspoon salt. Stir to coat the vegetables in the butter, then cook, stirring every so often, for about 15 minutes, until the vegetables are soft; lower the heat and add small splashes of water as needed to prevent any burning.

When the vegetables are soft, add the tomatoes and their juices, smooshing with a spoon to roughly break up the tomatoes. Add 1¼ cups (300ml) water, the fried beans, the reserved whole beans, the remaining 2 tablespoons butter, and ¾ teaspoon salt.

Bring the mixture to a simmer and cook for about 15 minutes, until it tastes full and round and delicious to you. Adjust the salt if needed.

go ahead, cut unevenly

Lots of recipes will tell you to cut vegetables evenly
so they cook evenly. Here's your permission to do
the opposite. Different sizes yield different textures
(picture: soft-caramelized versus crisp-tender),
adding more personality to this chili or any soup or
stew or stir-fry.

creamiest tomato soup without any cream

The answer to the creamiest tomato soup? Skip the cream. From a distance, this seems counterintuitive, illogical, unbelievable. But the answer comes by way of two other ingredients that just happen to be dairy-free: cashews and onions.

You've probably already heard of cashew cream, aka the easiest nut milk ever. Unlike almonds, cashews are soft enough that you don't need to soak them overnight. And while something like coconut milk tastes unavoidably coconutty, cashew cream just tastes *creamy*.

And so do onions. I first learned of onion-cream thanks to chef Grant Lee Crilly via our Genius Recipes column. The idea being: If you puree cooked onions, you end up with a cream look-a-like, ready to take dinner by storm. In this case, we simply sauté a lot of onions to start the soup. By the time everything gets buzzed together, you achieve a vegan cream of tomato that's even creamier and more savory than the original—though no one will quite know why.

Pour the cashews and 1½ cups (360ml) water into a blender to soak while you start the soup.

Set a stockpot over medium heat and add 4 tablespoons (60ml) of the oil. When the oil is hot, add the onions and 1 teaspoon salt. Cook, stirring occasionally, for 10 to 12 minutes, until the onions are translucent and soft—lower the heat as needed; we don't want them to brown.

Stir in the remaining 1 tablespoon oil and the tomato paste and cook, stirring frequently, for about 5 minutes, until the tomato paste is super fragrant and a rustier, deeper shade of red. (This means bigger, better tomato flavor.)

Deglaze the pot with 1 cup (240ml) water, scraping the bottom to release any caramelized bits. Add the whole peeled tomatoes, their juices, and 2 teaspoons salt. Simmer uncovered, stirring occasionally, for about 40 minutes, until the soup has thickened a bit and tastes very flavorful. Turn off the heat and use an immersion blender to blend until smooth.

Blend the cashews and water until smooth, then pour into the soup. Blend with the immersion blender again. Taste and adjust the salt if needed, and stir in more water if you want it thinner. This freezes beautifully.

SERVES 6

1⅓ cups (185g)
raw cashews

5 tablespoons (75ml)
extra-virgin olive oil

2 pounds (910g) yellow
onions, halved and
roughly chopped

Kosher salt

1 (6-ounce/170g) can
tomato paste

2 (28-ounce/795g)
cans whole
peeled tomatoes

french onion soup, but with leeks

French onion soup isn't actually about the onions. It's about the broth, the wine, and, best of all, the cheesy toast on top. This isn't to say that you can skip the vegetable matter; rather, you can swap in something like leeks and end up with a just-as-great soup. Leeks are part of the allium crew, with an herbier, grassier flavor than onions, almost like oversize chives. Their timing is a plus, too. Onions were born to be caramelized, which takes close to an hour if you're doing it right. Leeks, on the other hand, would rather stay green (they actually become more bitter when browned), which means you can have dinner on the table in a fraction of the time. While classic French onion soup calls for broth, usually beef, this opts for water. Just trust. Though this liquid starts out flavorless, between the leeks, garlic, and wine, it turns into a lovely broth in its own right. And speaking of wine: Pick a crisp variety that you'd want to drink on its own. You're going to have most of the bottle left over, so you might as well look forward to it.

SERVES 4

4 large leeks

¼ cup (55g) unsalted butter

5 large garlic cloves, minced

Kosher salt and freshly ground black pepper

⅔ cup (160ml) dry white wine

4 thick slices bread

4 ounces (115g) Gruyère, grated

Chop each leek in half crosswise, separating the green tops from the white bottoms. Lop off their hairy butts, halve the white parts lengthwise, and chop into 1-inch (2.5cm) half-moons. Cut the green parts into ½-inch (1.3cm) rounds. Wash and dry. (See tip opposite).

Melt the butter in a stockpot over medium heat, then add the garlic. Cook, stirring constantly, until the garlic starts to turn golden. Add the leeks, 2 teaspoons salt, and a pinch of pepper and toss with tongs to coat the leeks in the butter. Cover the pot and cook for about 5 minutes to wilt the leeks. Remove the lid and cook for another 6 to 12 minutes, stirring every so often and lowering the heat as needed to avoid browning, until the leeks are soft but still green. Pour in the wine and use a wooden spoon to scrape up any bits stuck to the bottom. Bring the wine to a simmer and cook for 1 minute, then pour in 5 cups (1.2L) water and add another 1 teaspoon salt. Bring to a simmer and cook for about 10 minutes.

While that's simmering, heat the broiler with a rack positioned in the upper part of the oven. Set the bread on a baking sheet and broil until toasty. Flip the bread and broil until the other side is toasty, then remove from the oven. Evenly divide the grated cheese on top of the toast, then broil again until the cheese is gooey and starting to char.

Taste the soup and season with salt and pepper if needed. Ladle it into four bowls, then float a piece of cheesy toast on top of each.

how to wash leeks like you mean it

Leeks are dirty, dirty creatures that love to hoard grit. To make sure you don't miss anything, treat them like lettuce. After chopping into pieces, add as many as will fit to a salad spinner. Fill with enough cold water to slosh around with your hands, then lift the strainer straight up and dump out the water (or use it to water houseplants). Repeat this until the water comes out clean enough to drink.

a fridge hero

There are many, many varieties of the Japanese fermented paste miso—depending on the main ingredients (say, soybeans and rice), as well as fermentation time. Creamy, mellow, sweet-ish white miso is my go-to for soups of all kinds, noodle and pasta sauces (see page 72), and salad dressings. In the recipe opposite, you can swap in a darker variety, like red miso, but start with half the quantity and adjust to taste from there.

charred carrot soup with miso

My back-pocket method for silky-smooth vegetable soup takes place, almost entirely, in the oven. Here's the cheat sheet: Roast vegetables, throw them in a blender with water and something-flavorful, press a button, and pat yourself on the back. (At this point, I usually container and freeze, then devour for lunch a couple of weeks or months down the road.) The trick is to take the vegetables farther in the oven than you think you should. The softer they are, the better they'll blend, and those charred, almost-burnt edges become a seasoning in their own right. Maybe the vegetables are parsnips and leeks, or broccoli and cauliflower. Maybe the flavor-booster is Worcestershire or cheddar. The options stretch as far as your eyes can see, but this is the combo I always come back to.

Heat the oven to 425°F (220°C). Combine the carrots, 1 tablespoon of the oil, and ¾ teaspoon salt on a rimmed baking sheet and mix. Combine the celery, onions, the remaining 2 tablespoons oil, and 1 teaspoon salt on another rimmed baking sheet and mix. Stick both pans in the oven and roast until the vegetables are fork-tender and dramatically browning in several spots, 40 to 60 minutes total, shuffling the vegetables with a spatula halfway through to encourage even cooking.

Add half of the cooked carrots, celery, and onions to a blender along with 3 tablespoons of the miso and 4 cups (950ml) water. Blend until smooth, then pour into a stockpot. Repeat with the remaining vegetables, the remaining 3 tablespoons miso, and another 4 cups (950ml) water.

Give the soup a taste. Add more salt, water, or miso until it's highly cozy to you. If needed, warm over medium-low heat, stirring every so often, until it's however hot you like your soup. (Alternatively, after you blend it, you can stick it in the fridge or freezer for another day.)

SERVES 6

2 pounds (910g) carrots, peeled and chopped into 1-inch (2.5cm) chunks

3 tablespoons neutral oil

Kosher salt

1 pound (455g) celery, chopped into 1-inch (2.5cm) chunks

1 pound (455g) yellow onions, halved, peeled, and cut into 1-inch (2.5cm) chunks

6 tablespoons (105g) white miso, plus more to taste

stop taking stock so seriously

Most chicken stock recipes call for a lot more than chicken. Just like most beef stock recipes call for a lot more than beef, and most mushroom stock recipes call for a lot more than mushrooms. The technical term for this is aromatics, a catch-all for vegetables (like onions, carrots, and celery), herbs (like parsley, thyme, and bay leaves), and spices (like peppercorns and coriander). The theory being: Aromatics round out stock, creating more complex flavor. This is true. But aromatics don't create chickenier—or beefier or mushroomier—flavor. And isn't that what we came for?

It's easy to see how boxed stock and cubed bouillon became so popular in home kitchens. With a flock of ingredients and techniques (bouquet garni? egg white raft? what?), from-scratch stock seems intimidating. But it doesn't have to be. Think of stock less like kombucha and more like tea: water steeped with something to become something else. The sort of thing to make on a whim. All of the recipes here hinge on one ingredient plus water and salt. Some take a matter of minutes; others are a by-product of another dish. You can use immediately, or refrigerate for up to 1 week, or freeze for up to 3 months.

mushroom

YIELD: 1 ½ QUARTS (1.4L)

Think of mushroom stock as beef stock without the beef—sultry and brawny with confident umami. While meat stocks can eat up an entire day on the stove, shelf-stable dried shiitakes deliver that low-and-slow flavor in the length of a sitcom. Use this for last-minute soup, risotto, or vegetarian gravy.

Combine 2 quarts (1.9L) water and 10 to 15 (13 to 20g) whole dried shiitakes in a pot. Set over high heat, partially cover, and bring to a boil. Drop to a simmer, cook for 20 minutes, then cut the heat. Drain (but save the mushrooms for anywhere you'd use mushrooms). At this point, you can season with kosher salt to taste (I add about 2 teaspoons), or season later on.

bitter greens

YIELD: 2 QUARTS (1.9L)

Repeat after me: Do not throw out blanching liquid. Even if a vegetable cooks only for a matter of minutes, loud-voiced ingredients—looking at you, broccoli rabe—still leave an impression. Use some of this as a home for white beans, plus those blanched greens and a long pour of olive oil. Then use the rest anywhere that calls for vegetable stock.

Add 2 quarts (1.9L) water to a pot and bring to a boil. Stir in 2 teaspoons kosher salt and 1 bunch roughly chopped broccoli rabe. Cook for about 5 minutes, then use tongs or a sieve to remove the broccoli rabe. Taste the stock and add more salt if needed.

kombu

YIELD: SCANT 2 QUARTS (1.9L)

In Japanese cooking, dashi is an all-purpose broth used for soups, sauces, seasoning, and more. While the most popular iteration calls for kombu and bonito flakes, that little ingredient list can get even littler by using only kombu instead. This flavor-packed dried seaweed can be found at Asian grocers, many American supermarkets, and online. Store it in a cool, dry place.

Combine 2 pieces (about 4 square inches/ 10 square cm each) kombu with 2 quarts (1.9L) water in a stockpot. Cover and let soak at room temperature for 2 to 10 hours. At this point, remove the lid, transfer the pot to the stove, and bring to a gentle simmer. Cook for about 15 minutes, until the flavor is wonderful to you. Strain out the kombu and season the stock with kosher salt to taste (a scant 2 teaspoons for me), or season later on.

Note: That spent kombu can be used to make a milder, secondary dashi (niban dashi): Combine the leftover kombu with 6 cups (1.4L) water and simmer for about 10 minutes.

garlic

YIELD: 2 QUARTS (1.9L)

Savory and nourishing with a just-right amount of attitude, garlic stock, like chicken stock, is wonderful to slurp from a mug whenever you're feeling not 100 percent. Beyond that, use it in bean stews, vegetarian French onion soup (page 42), any-dumpling soup (from pork wontons to matzo balls), and boiled grains (rice, quinoa, polenta, etc.).

Peel 2 big heads garlic (tips on how to do this without losing your mind on page 89). Roughly chop the cloves. Combine with 12 cups (2.8L) water in a stockpot and bring to a boil over high heat. Lower the heat to a confident simmer and cook for 1 hour or so, until the liquid has reduced to about 8 cups (1.9L). Pour through a fine-mesh sieve into a heatproof bowl. Use a spoon to mash the softened garlic through the sieve, enriching the broth (I incorporate almost all of it, but it's your broth). Season with kosher salt to taste (1½ to 2 teaspoons for me), or season later on.

But wait! Even more one-ingredient stocks:

parmesan (page 50)   bean (page 55)

corn cob (page 52)   chicken (page 56)

cream of mushroom soup with just cream & mushrooms

Beyond the two namesake ingredients, most cream of mushroom soup recipes call for other vegetables (like onions, shallots, and celery), fresh or dried herbs (like thyme, tarragon, and bay leaves), stock or broth, red or white wine, and sometimes a thickener (like flour or cornstarch). We don't need any of that. Fresh baby bella (aka cremini) mushrooms have a meaty—even beefy— flavor and modest price. And dried shiitakes effortlessly transmogrify water (just ask the stock on page 46) before getting blended into oblivion. After you pour the cream into the sautéing mushrooms, be sure to really *scraaape* the bottom of the pot. Those stuck, crusty bits are half the reason the ingredient list is so small. Pair with a vinegary salad or warm bread or both.

SERVES 2 TO 3

9 whole
dried shiitakes

2 tablespoons
unsalted butter

1½ pounds (685g) baby
bella mushrooms,
thinly sliced

Kosher salt and freshly
ground black pepper

1 cup (240ml) heavy
cream, plus more
for drizzling

Combine 3 cups (720ml) water and the shiitakes in a pot and set over high heat. Bring to a boil, cook for 5 minutes, then turn off the heat.

Add the butter to a wide, high-sided saucepan and set over medium heat. Once the butter melts, add the baby bellas. Cook, stirring occasionally, for 15 to 20 minutes, until they are sticking to the bottom and deeply browning. (At first they'll release a lot of liquid, but it'll evaporate.)

Season the baby bellas with 1 teaspoon salt and ½ teaspoon pepper and stir. Remove ½ cup (80g) and set aside on a plate. (These will become our garnish.) Now add the cream to the saucepan and scrape up the browned bits on the bottom. Simmer for a few minutes until the cream slightly thickens and turns the color of chocolate milk.

Add the creamy mushroom mixture to a blender, along with the shiitakes and their water (pour slowly so you don't include the grit at the bottom).

With the keyhole of the blender lid open and a kitchen towel pressed on top, blend until smooth. Taste and adjust the seasoning as needed. If you'd like the soup to be thinner, just add a splash of water or cream.

Serve the soup with the browned mushrooms sprinkled on top, plus a drizzle of cream if you want.

parmesan broth

MAKES 6 CUPS (1.4L)

12 ounces (340g) Parmigiano-
Reggiano rinds, chopped into
1- to 2-inch (2.5 to 5cm) pieces

Kosher salt

Combine 2 quarts (1.9L) water and
the Parmesan rinds in a large pot
over medium-high heat. Bring to
a boil, then lower the heat and
simmer for about 1½ hours, stirring
every so often so the cheese
doesn't stick to the bottom, until
super flavorful and reduced to
about 6 cups (1.4L).

Strain the broth into a heatproof
container and season with salt to
taste. The stock will keep in the
refrigerator for several days, or
in the freezer for several weeks.
Thaw and warm over low heat
before using.

garlicky escarole toast in parmesan broth

I could tell you to grate your own Parmigiano-Reggiano because the flavor is better, or because you can fine-tune the coarseness however you want. But the real reason you should grate your own Parm is: It comes with a rind. Yep, that thing you've probably been throwing out. Collect rinds over a month or two—the Eggplant Parm on page 121 is ready to help—and tuck them in the freezer until you have enough for this recipe. When simmered for a couple hours, they turn tap water into the umami-est broth, into liquid gold, into the elixir of life. You can make the broth in advance, stick it in the freezer, and put it toward a million meals: Blend with roasted vegetables, especially parsnips, for an ultra-creamy creamless soup. Stir in white miso, then add cooked beans and kale. But before you do any of that, make this garlicky escarole toast to float in it.

Heat the oil in a large pot over medium heat. Add the chopped garlic and sauté, stirring constantly, until it starts to turn lightly golden. Add the escarole and a big pinch each of salt and pepper. Use tongs to toss, coating the escarole in the oil. Cover and cook for a few minutes to wilt the leaves, then uncover and cook another few minutes, until tender.

Turn off the heat and stir in the grated Parm. Taste and add more salt, pepper, and cheese until you love it.

Set a cast-iron skillet over medium heat and add a couple of glugs of oil to cover the bottom of the pan. When the oil is hot, add as many slices of bread as will fit. Toast for a few minutes, until the bottom is golden brown and crispy, then flip and repeat on the other side, adding more oil if the skillet looks dry. As soon as you remove the bread from the pan, rub it on both sides with the whole garlic clove, then sprinkle with salt and pepper. Repeat with any remaining slices.

To serve, distribute the toasts among four shallow bowls and evenly divide the escarole on top. Pour 1½ cups (360ml) of the broth around each toast and shower with grated Parm.

SERVES 4

6 tablespoons (90ml) extra-virgin olive oil, plus more for the bread

12 garlic cloves (11 roughly chopped, 1 left whole)

2 heads escarole, roughly chopped, washed, and dried

Kosher salt and freshly ground black pepper

½ cup (50g) finely grated Parmigiano-Reggiano, plus more for topping

8 thick slices crusty bread (like sourdough)

Parmesan Broth, hot (see recipe opposite)

spicy corn soup with shiitakes & green onions

It's well known that if you roast a chicken, you should put the bones toward a pot of water, where they will simmer—and simmer and simmer—until that liquid turns into gold. The same, it turns out, can be said of corncobs. From a distance, these seem good for little more than the compost bin. But! There is a load of sweet, summery flavor to be drawn out. Less than an hour yields a stock cheery enough to salt and slurp as is, which is good news for any corn soup or stew, from American chowder to Cantonese egg drop. In this version, after the cobs get off work, the vegetables themselves (juicy corn, slippery mushrooms, herby green onions) take a swift dunk—less to cook through, more to warm up while staying sprightly. A shake of whatever hot sauce you love (read: is already in your fridge) adds both kick and acidity to counter all the corny sweetness. My go-to is Cholula's Green Pepper. Serve the soup with something starchy, like steamed grains or warm bread.

SERVES 4

4 ears corn, husked

2 teaspoons hot sauce, plus more to taste

Kosher salt

8 ounces (225g) shiitakes, thinly sliced

1 bunch green onions

Use a sharp chef's knife to cut the corn kernels from the cobs. Add the naked cobs to a stockpot along with 8 cups (1.9L) water. Bring to a boil, then reduce to a lively simmer and cook for 30 to 45 minutes, until the liquid has reduced to 5 cups (1.2L) and tastes corny. At this point, cut the heat and remove and discard the cobs. Stir in the hot sauce and 1 teaspoon salt, then adjust both to taste.

Bring the seasoned broth back to a simmer and stir in the corn kernels and mushrooms. Cook for about 5 minutes, until the mushrooms have significantly wilted and the corn is crisp-tender. Meanwhile, thinly slice the green onions and stir them in to wilt. Season with salt and hot sauce to taste.

brothy white beans with broccoli rabe & pepperoni

While the liquid in a can of beans is good for little more than pouring down the drain (or making vegan meringue, but that's a conversation for another day), the liquid in a pot of just-cooked beans is a cozy, nourishing, slurp-worthy broth. To turn this into soup, you could add lots of different things, like vegetables, spices, herbs, and wine. Or you could add two: bitter greens and salty cured meat. The former could be escarole, kale, arugula, or, in our case, broccoli rabe. Once finely chopped, it wilts almost instantly, infusing the broth with tons of bright green flavor. The pepperoni—or, if you prefer, Spanish chorizo, hard salami, or even vegan sausage—comes in at the end. Pan-frying slices not only turns them crunchy like bacon but also yields a pseudo–chile oil for enriching the soup.

Give the beans a quick sort to get rid of any unwanted bits, then add to a stockpot, cover with cold water by 2 inches (5cm), and stir in 2 tablespoons of the salt. Cover the pot and let soak for 8 to 12 hours.

When the beans are ready, drain and rinse them. Return them to the pot and add 10 cups (2.4L) cold water plus 1 teaspoon of the salt. Partially cover the pot and set it over medium heat to come to a simmer. Cook, stirring occasionally and adjusting the heat as needed to maintain a simmer, for 45 minutes to 1½ hours, until the beans are creamy and tender.

While the beans cook, prep the broccoli rabe: Thinly slice the stems and roughly chop the leaves, then wash and dry (see page 43 for tips).

When the beans are done, gently stir in the remaining 1 teaspoon salt and the broccoli rabe, and cook until the stems are crisp-tender and the broth tastes vegetal, 3 to 4 minutes. Turn the heat to its lowest setting to stay warm while you crisp the pepperoni.

Put a large cast-iron or nonstick skillet over medium heat and add just enough oil to thinly coat the bottom. Add the pepperoni and cook for 2 to 4 minutes, flipping halfway through, until the slices are crispy-edged and browned. Transfer the pepperoni to a plate, then pour the spiced oil into a heatproof bowl or glass.

Ladle the soup into bowls. Top with crispy pepperoni and a big drizzle of the spiced oil.

SERVES 6

1 pound (455g) dried cannellini beans (or a similar variety)

2 tablespoons plus 2 teaspoons kosher salt

1 bunch broccoli rabe

Extra-virgin olive oil

9 ounces (255g) hard pepperoni, thinly sliced into coins (about 2 cups)

chicken noodle soup with lots of dill

When I was growing up, my mom made chicken soup on three occasions: Jewish holidays, whenever my brother or I was sick, and the first day of school. It had matzo balls, egg noodles, shredded meat, carrot, celery, onion, parsley, and dill, plus an ice cube so I wouldn't burn my tongue. My own version is lazier, but just as comforting.

While some cooks cherry-pick specific chicken parts, say wings or backs, I like the all-in-one flavor of a whole bird, and the mix of white and dark meat. (To save some cleanup, you can kindly ask your butcher to cut up the chicken for you.)

Because there's so much dill (please and thank you), buying by the bunch, versus pre-packaged containers, is your best bet. If that's not possible, feel free to swap in parsley. You might want to break up the stock over a couple of days. Chilling it, then skimming the fat gives you the most control when it comes to seasoning. That said, there have been many occasions when I want chicken soup *now*, and I just spoon off some fat while it's still warm. Yes, this is less efficient, and, yes, the soup ends up significantly schmaltz-ier. Sometimes this is just what we need.

SERVES 4

1 (5½-pound/2.5kg) chicken

Kosher salt

12 ounces (340g) extra-wide egg noodles

1½ cups (60g) roughly chopped dill plus ¾ cup (40g) finely chopped dill

Take a peek inside your chicken—there's probably a bag with the neck and giblets. Reserve the neck and toss the rest (or freeze for later). Use a cleaver or chef's knife to cut the chicken into 8 to 12 roughly equal pieces. Add those, plus the neck, to a stockpot. Pour 12 cups (2.8L) water on top. Partially cover the pot and set over high heat to come to a simmer. Cook, adjusting the heat as needed to maintain a simmer, for about 25 minutes, until the meat is cooked through (165°F/75°C). If any scum rises to the surface, use a spoon to skim and discard it.

Use tongs to transfer the chicken pieces to a baking sheet. When the meat is cool enough to handle, use your hands to pull the meat from the bones. Season the chicken with salt, transfer it to a container, and refrigerate. Add all the bones and skin back to the pot.

With the pot partially covered, simmer the stock for 2½ to 4 hours, until golden and reduced to about 8 cups (1.9L) of liquid. Check every so often to make sure it's simmering, not boiling.

When the stock is ready, pour it through a fine-mesh sieve into a heatproof vessel, then press on the bones to squeeze out every last drop. You can skim some fat from the top while the stock is warm, end up with a richer broth, and start the noodles right away. Or cool to room temperature, then refrigerate until completely chilled. (This will take several hours.) When chilled, the stock will be gelatinous like jelly. Use a spoon to skim the opaque fat from the top and transfer it to a jar in the fridge.

When you're ready to eat, set a large pot of water over high heat. Once it boils, generously season it with salt. Add the noodles and cook for about 4 minutes, until not quite al dente (they'll continue to cook in the soup).

Meanwhile, heat the stock in a separate pot over medium-high heat. Shred the chicken by hand. If you're using all of the stock, you'll want about 4½ cups (1 pound/455g) of shredded chicken for four bowls of soup. (This means you'll have some leftover chicken; save for sandwiches.)

Season the hot broth with 2 teaspoons salt. If you chilled and skimmed the broth, stir in 1 tablespoon of the reserved chicken fat. Taste and adjust the salt and fat until you love it. Stir in the shredded chicken.

When the noodles are done, use a slotted spoon to divide them among four soup bowls, then add the dill, broth, and shredded chicken.

pastas, grains & bready things

bacon & eggs spaghetti

In *The Essentials of Italian Cooking*, Marcella Hazan writes about the rumored history of carbonara: "During the last days of World War II, American soldiers in Rome who had made friends with local families would bring them eggs and bacon and ask them to turn them into pasta sauce." Naturally, this meant adding cheese, be it Parmigiano-Reggiano or Pecorino or both. But what if they had just stuck with eggs, bacon, and pasta? They'd get something like this. Buttery egg yolks, warm bacon fat, and starchy water are more than capable of creating a silky sauce all on their own. And while it's by no means traditional, I like to add a bonus egg on top—crackly-edged and ready to ooze everywhere at the touch of a fork.

Add 5 cups (1.2L) water to a small pot and bring to a boil. Season with ½ teaspoon salt. Add the spaghetti, encouraging it into the water, and cook for 7 to 8 minutes, until al dente.

Meanwhile, add the bacon to a cast-iron skillet over medium heat. Cook for about 7 minutes, flipping halfway through, until it's as crunchy as you like. Transfer to a plate and pour almost all of the fat into a heatproof measuring cup, leaving about 1 tablespoon in the pan.

With the heat still at medium, crack 2 eggs into the skillet and sprinkle with salt and pepper. Cook until the whites are set but the yolks are still runny.

Combine the egg yolks and the remaining egg in a medium heatproof bowl, season with ½ teaspoon pepper, and beat with a fork. While stirring, slowly drizzle in the reserved bacon fat to temper the yolks.

When the spaghetti is almost done, drop the heat to medium-low, and scoop out ⅔ cup (160ml) pasta water with the emptied heatproof measuring cup. While stirring, slowly drizzle half of the pasta water into the egg–bacon fat mixture. Use tongs to add the spaghetti.

Set the bowl over the pot. The bowl should be hovering above the simmering water (discard or add water if needed). Use tongs to toss the spaghetti until the sauce becomes creamy and thick enough to cling to the noodles, adding more pasta water to sight.

Divide the saucy spaghetti between two plates. Top each with an egg, half the bacon, and more black pepper.

SERVES 2

Kosher salt

8 ounces (225g) spaghetti

4 thick slices bacon, halved crosswise

3 large eggs

Freshly ground black pepper

3 large egg yolks

scorched rice with avocado & horseradish tahini

There's a lot of precedent for purposefully scorched rice: Dominican concón, Korean nurungji, Persian tahdig, Senegalese xoon, Spanish socarrat, and the list goes on. This rice bowl is kindled by that technique and its crunchy-fluffy contrast. Just a slick of oil and a few minutes in a hot skillet transform cooked rice (I like brown for its bonus flavor but, yes, you can swap in white) from tender to cracker-esque. It's a habit-forming way to spruce up an otherwise-soft grain bowl, whether you're donning it with ripe avocado and a sinus-clearing horseradish sauce, or a soft-boiled egg and vinegared greens, or, really, whatever you want.

SERVES 4

1¼ cups (225g) short-grain brown rice, rinsed

Kosher salt

1 teaspoon plus
1 tablespoon neutral oil

2 large ripe avocados

Double-batch
Horseradish Tahini
(page 35)

Lemon wedges
(optional)

Add the rice to a pot with 2⅓ cups (545ml) water and a pinch of salt, and set over medium-high heat. As soon as the water boils, cover the pot, reduce the heat to low, and cook for 40 minutes. Remove the pot from the heat but leave it covered for 10 minutes. Uncover and fluff the rice with a fork. Transfer 1 cup (170g) of the rice to a bowl. Season the rice left in the pot with salt if needed and cover the pot to keep warm.

To make the scorched rice, stir 1 teaspoon of the oil into the bowl of rice, and add the remaining 1 tablespoon oil to a large nonstick skillet over medium heat. Once the oil is hot, add the oiled rice and spread it flat. Cook for 5 to 8 minutes, not stirring at all, until the rice is crispy and popcorn-scented and the grains are starting to separate like lace. Use a silicone or wooden spatula to flip the rice. Toast for another 30 seconds just to kiss the other side, then transfer to a towel-lined plate. Let it cool, then break it into shards with your hands.

Halve the avocados and discard the pits. Peel away the avocado skin and cut the flesh into slices, chunks, or both.

Divide the fluffy rice among four bowls, then evenly top with the avocado and scorched rice. Serve with the horseradish tahini for everyone to spoon on top, plus lemon wedges if you'd like.

a ripe avocado is hard to find

This fruit ripens off the vine and does so at its own pace. But these tricks help: If your avocado is a rock and you want a rice bowl soon, put it in a brown bag along with some bananas; they'll encourage each other. And if your avocado is tender (gingerly press the spot by the stem to check), but you aren't ready to eat it for a day or more, stick it in the fridge to slow the ripening.

bow ties with anchovy butter, kale & kasha

My grandma's second husband's favorite dinner was kasha varnishkes—or, as I like to call it, kash varn. Half of the ingredient list is in the name: Kasha refers to roasted buckwheat groats, while varnishkes nods to bow-tie noodles (aka farfalle in Italian). Lots of sautéed onions and schmaltz get involved. It's classic Jewish comfort food.

    This version though? Decidedly un-classic. I keep the namesake ingredients—truly, you can't beat carbs on carbs—but dress them up with some new accessories. Instead of onions, ruffly kale adds some much-needed greenery. And instead of chicken fat, I smash mighty anchovies into soft butter.

    Toasting kasha in fat, then boiling it is a traditional strategy to keep the grains separate. We'll do that. But we'll also *keep* toasting even more kasha, until it starts to split and puff and smell like toast, yielding a crunchy topping to sprinkle with abandon. When you buy the kasha, make sure you get whole-grain, not medium- or fine-grain.

Fill a stockpot with water and set over high heat to come to a boil.

Meanwhile, slice the kale crosswise into thin-as-possible ribbons and add to a big bowl. Combine 5 tablespoons (75g) of the butter and the anchovies in a small bowl and mash with a fork until smoothish.

Melt 2 tablespoons (30g) of the butter in a cast-iron or nonstick skillet over medium heat. Add the kasha and stir. Cook for 5 minutes, stirring occasionally and lowering the heat if the groats are darkening too quickly, until the kasha is toasty. Dump the kasha into a bowl but leave the heat on. Add the remaining 1 tablespoon (15g) butter to the emptied skillet along with ⅔ cup (120g) of that just-toasted kasha. Continue to cook, stirring often, until the kasha starts to split like popcorn, 3 to 5 minutes. Transfer the kasha to a plate and sprinkle with salt; this will be our crunchy topping.

When the water reaches a boil, lightly season it with salt (since anchovies are salty). Add the pasta and set a timer for 3 minutes. When that goes off, add the larger portion of kasha and set a timer for 7 minutes. When that goes off, use a sieve to transfer the pasta and kasha to the bowl with the kale. Toss to wilt the kale, then add the anchovy butter and keep tossing until it melts. Taste and add salt or pasta water if needed. Top with the crispy kasha and give one more toss, so some gets incorporated but most stays on top.

SERVES 4

2 bunches Tuscan kale, stems removed

½ cup (120g) unsalted butter, at room temperature

2 (2-ounce/55g) tins oil-packed anchovy fillets, drained and minced

2 cups (360g) kasha

Kosher salt

12 ounces (340g) bow-tie pasta (farfalle)

flatbread with beet yogurt & greens

I used to wake up at 2 a.m. and bake bread for a living, which explains why, now that I no longer work at a bakery, I have next to no interest in making from-scratch loaves for fun. This flatbread is a happy exception. It doesn't require a sourdough starter or even yeast, but it delivers the same warm, crusty, downy satisfaction with three staple ingredients—one of which, yogurt, comes in handy twice: It lends a sourdough twang and pillowy crumb to the flatbread (as in many versions of Indian naan and Turkish bazlama). And it whirls into a tangy, vegetal beet dip, much like Persian borani, with a color so vibrant you might have to shield your eyes.

SERVES 4

flatbread

2 cups (250g) white whole-wheat flour, plus more for rolling

2 teaspoons baking powder

1 teaspoon kosher salt, plus more for sprinkling

½ cup (120g) whole-milk Greek yogurt

Extra-virgin olive oil

beet greens & yogurt

2 bunches beets, preferably 1 red and 1 golden, with their greens

3 tablespoons extra-virgin olive oil

Kosher salt

1¼ cups (300g) whole-milk Greek yogurt

Heat the oven to 400°F (200°C).

To make the flatbread dough, combine the flour, baking powder, and salt in a bowl. Mix the yogurt with ½ cup (120ml) water in a smaller bowl, then pour this into the dry ingredients. Stir until nearly cohesive, then finish bringing it together by hand in the bowl, adding more water if needed; the dough should be slightly sticky but not wet. Cover the bowl and let the dough hang out while you work on the beets.

Use a knife to separate the beets from their tops and remove any tails, then scrub the beets under water. Transfer them to a baking dish and season with 1 tablespoon of the oil and 1 teaspoon salt. Pour ¼ cup (60ml) water around the beets. Cover the dish with aluminum foil and roast for 40 to 60 minutes, until the beets are knife-tender.

Meanwhile, tear the leaves off the beet stems and individually wash both. Roughly chop the stems and leaves, keeping them separate.

Set a large skillet over medium heat and add the remaining 2 tablespoons oil. When the oil is hot, add the stems and a big pinch of salt. Cook, stirring occasionally, until the stems start to get tender, about 4 minutes. Add the greens and cook, tossing constantly, until they're just wilted, about 1 minute more. Turn off the heat and partially cover.

To cook the flatbread, heat a cast-iron skillet over medium heat. Divide the dough into four equal pieces. On a lightly floured surface, roll one piece into a 7 by 6-inch (18 by 15cm) rectangle. Add enough oil to cover the bottom of the skillet. When it's hot, carefully add the shaped flatbread dough. Cook for 1½ to 2½ minutes, until the bottom is deeply golden brown and charring in spots. Flip, pressing down on the bubbles to flatten if needed, and cook for another 1½ to 2½ minutes, until deeply golden brown on the second side. Sprinkle with salt if you'd like.

Transfer to a wire rack or keep it warm in the turned-off oven after the beets are done. Repeat with the remaining flatbreads, adding additional oil as needed.

To make the beet yogurt, peel one of the red beets and roughly chop enough to yield a heaping ⅓ cup (about 60g). Pulse in a food processor until finely minced. Scrape down the sides of the processor, add the yogurt and ¼ teaspoon salt, and puree until silky smooth and bright fuchsia.

Peel and cut the remaining beets into wedges and rounds for varied textures. Serve these with their pan juices, the sautéed greens and stems, flatbread, and beet yogurt. You can layer the flatbread like a pizza or tear it into pieces and mix and match as you go. Any leftover yogurt makes an excellent afternoon snack.

cheesy quinoa fritters with lemony endive

Alice Waters is known for farm-to-table cooking, especially salads. Arguably her most famous involves goat cheese with garden lettuces—dreamed up in the '80s at Chez Panisse—hinging on custardy cheese, crispy breading, and barely dressed greens. That never gets old. This riff borrows the idea but streamlines one step. Instead of coating goat cheese in bread crumbs, I take a breezier path: stirring the cheese into fluffy quinoa, which transforms into a crunchy-as-heck crust when pan-fried. As for the salad, any lettuce that adds some spring to your step works—for me, that's snappy endive, which looks like flower petals when you pull it apart. If that's not your thing, try baby arugula or radicchio or watercress. What's important is that you pick just one and let it speak for itself.

In a medium pot over medium-high heat, combine the quinoa, 2 cups (480ml) water, and ½ teaspoon salt. Bring to a boil, then drop the heat to low, cover the pot, and simmer for about 15 minutes, until the quinoa is fluffy and tender, and the water has been absorbed.

Add the cheese to the hot quinoa and stir until melted. Season with a big pinch each of salt and pepper. Spread the mixture onto a plate and refrigerate for about 15 minutes to firm up.

Form into 16 patties (a scant 2 tablespoons each). Refrigerate, covered, for at least 15 minutes or up to 2 days—this helps them hold their shape.

Set a cast-iron or nonstick skillet over medium heat. Add enough oil to thinly coat the bottom. When the oil is hot, add 6 to 8 quinoa patties with ample room in between. Pan-fry for about 4 minutes, until their bottoms are deeply golden brown. Carefully flip and fry for another 3 to 4 minutes, until the second side is deeply golden brown. Transfer the patties to a wire rack, and cook the remaining patties.

Chop off the very bottom of the endives and discard. Pull apart the leaves, trimming the bottom core into rounds along the way; save these coins for the salad too—they're delicious. Once you get to the core where the leaves are reluctant to separate, halve it lengthwise.

Throw the endive into a bowl and drizzle with oil and lemon juice, plus a pinch each of salt and pepper. Toss, taste, and adjust as needed.

Serve the fritters on top of the salad with lemon wedges on the side.

SERVES 4

1 cup (175g) white quinoa, rinsed

Kosher salt

6 ounces (170g) plain goat cheese

Freshly ground black pepper

Extra-virgin olive oil

4 Belgian endives

Freshly squeezed lemon juice, plus wedges for serving

how to make grilled cheese, the perfect food, perfect-er

Every few months, I make a ginormous batch of tomato soup (page 41), freeze it in quarts, and pull it out whenever I want grilled cheese for dinner. Whenever, it turns out, is almost every week. At its simplest, this sandwich needs no more than three ingredients: white bread, American cheese, and mayo all around (its lower smoke point sidesteps burnt bread). But, since this recipe is so simple to begin with, there's room to play around. Swap out a usual suspect for a new favorite, or add a bonus ingredient or two. Dare we? We dare.

bread   +   **spread**   +
                  [optional]

inside-out everything bagel

cinnamon raisin

croissant

focaccia

challah

flatbread (page 66)

pumpernickel

rye-caraway

english muffin

pesto

white miso

jam

honey

tapenade

harissa

nut or seed butter

prepared horseradish

whole-grain mustard

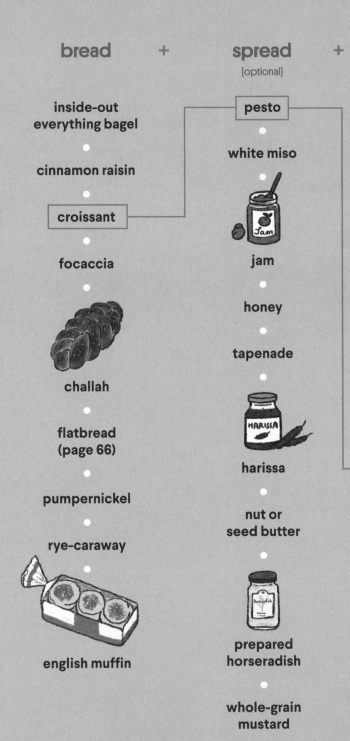

cheese	+	bulk	+	mayo		highly recommended combos

cheese + **bulk** [optional] + **mayo** [add-ins optional]

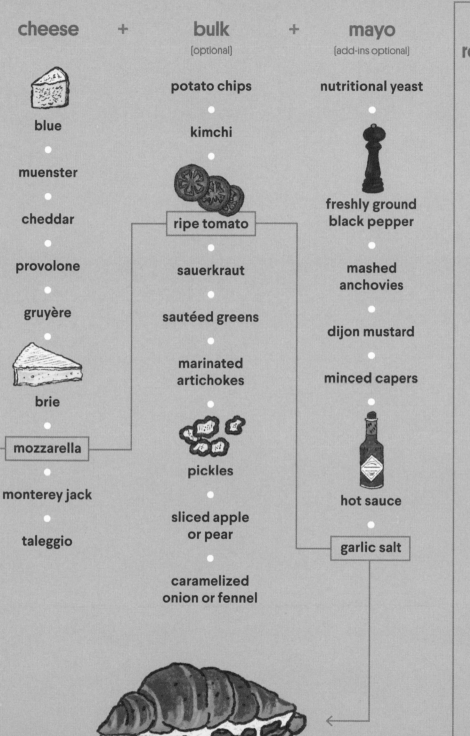

cheese

- blue
- muenster
- cheddar
- provolone
- gruyère
- brie
- mozzarella
- monterey jack
- taleggio

bulk [optional]

- potato chips
- kimchi
- ripe tomato
- sauerkraut
- sautéed greens
- marinated artichokes
- pickles
- sliced apple or pear
- caramelized onion or fennel

mayo [add-ins optional]

- nutritional yeast
- freshly ground black pepper
- mashed anchovies
- dijon mustard
- minced capers
- hot sauce
- garlic salt

highly recommended combos

pumpernickel
+
apricot jam
+
blue cheese

---

rye-caraway
+
muenster
+
sauerkraut

---

focaccia
+
taleggio
+
artichokes

---

croissant
+
honey
+
brie
+
dijon-mayo

---

challah
+
cheddar
+
potato chips
+
garlic-mayo

rigatoni with corn sauce & sizzled corn

For the corniest creamed corn, skip the cream altogether. Not in favor of half-and-half or even whole milk—but *corn milk*, that starchy sap that seeps from the cobs. This creamy but creamless pasta boasts a miso-smooched, sunny-colored sauce that hugs the noodles much like an Alfredo. Even more corn—honestly, come summer, you can never have too much—gets crisped in a skillet until it starts to snap, crackle, and pop all over your kitchen (naked forearms beware), for a crunchy, bread crumbish topping. For more ways to use up that jar of miso, stroll over to page 44.

SERVES 4

6 ears corn, shucked

3 tablespoons white miso

3 tablespoons unsalted butter, at room temperature (or neutral oil to make it vegan)

Kosher salt

1 pound (455g) rigatoni

Freshly ground black pepper or red pepper flakes (optional)

Fill a stockpot with water and set over high heat to come to a boil.

Use a chef's knife to cut the kernels off the corn; set the kernels aside. Now use the blunt edge of your knife to scrape the naked cobs, yielding a milky mush on your cutting board. Transfer that mush to a blender along with the miso, 2 tablespoons of the butter, and a pinch of salt.

Set a large cast-iron skillet over medium heat and add the remaining 1 tablespoon butter. When that's melted, add half of the kernels and a pinch of salt. Cook, stirring occasionally, until the corn is toasty and browned, 5 to 7 minutes. Turn off the heat.

When the water reaches a boil, generously season it with salt. Add the remaining raw kernels and cook for 2 minutes. Use a slotted spoon or spider to transfer the kernels to the blender. (Keep the water over high heat; we're using it again in a second.) Process the kernels until smooth, then season with salt to taste. Cover the blender to keep the mixture warm.

When the water returns to a boil, add the rigatoni. Cook for 8 to 14 minutes, until al dente. Turn off the heat and drain.

Combine the drained pasta and miso-corn sauce in the emptied stockpot and toss. Season with salt to taste—be generous here to balance the sweetness—then transfer to a platter or plates. Top with the crispy corn. You can add black pepper or red pepper flakes if you want, but I like to let the corn shine on its own.

lend me an ear

Even though it's a summer vegetable, corn comes with its own outerwear, making it all the harder to tell a good ear from a bad one. Here's what to look for when you're at the market: Husks that are bright green, not dull or dried out, with tassels that are fluffy, not swampy. If you take a peek inside, the kernels should be juicy and plump, not deflated or wrinkly, and in orderly rows, not all over the place.

wheat berries with mushrooms, sauerkraut & gouda

Chewy in texture and bronzed in color, wheat berries harbor the grain's bran, germ, and endosperm—which is to say, flavor, flavor, and more flavor. And while this ingredient takes some time to cook, you can 100 percent do this step in advance (say on a sleepy Sunday), store it in the fridge for several days, and use it whenever you're ready to rumble. From that point, it's a snappy weeknight meal. Cooking any grain twice—simmer to start, sauté to finish—yields a dish that's more than the sum of its parts. Especially with heavyweight mix-ins, like mushrooms and sauerkraut. German for "sour cabbage," the latter adds roughage, but also a plucky-tangy boost from all the earthiness. If you can't track down aged gouda, whose crystally texture and buttery flavor are earned in years, an elderly cheddar will do the trick.

Pour 8 cups (1.9L) water into a large pot and set over high heat. When it reaches a boil, add the wheat berries and ½ teaspoon salt. Simmer uncovered, adjusting the heat and adding water if needed, for 65 to 90 minutes, until the wheat berries are chewy-tender. Drain if necessary. (At this point, you can use the wheat berries immediately or refrigerate them in an airtight container for several days.)

Add 2 tablespoons of the butter to a large (at least 12-inch/30cm) cast-iron or nonstick skillet over medium heat. Once the butter has melted and is starting to foam, add the mushrooms and toss to coat. Cook, stirring occasionally, until the mushrooms have released their liquid and are starting to stick to the pan, 8 to 10 minutes. Sprinkle with salt.

Add the remaining 2 tablespoons butter to the skillet. Once the butter has melted, add the wheat berries. Mix to combine, then press the wheat berries into a flat layer. Cook over medium to medium-high (depending on the temperature of your wheat berries) for 8 to 12 minutes—shuffling then pressing back down a couple of times along the way—until the wheat berries are crisp, starting to crackle, and taste toasty. Stir in the sauerkraut just to warm it up, then turn off the heat. Season to taste with salt and/or more sauerkraut and its brine.

Divide the mixture among four plates and top each with gouda. Leave any extra cheese on the table so everyone can add more as they eat.

SERVES 4

1¼ cups (225g) wheat berries

Kosher salt

¼ cup (55g) unsalted butter

1 pound (455g) baby bella mushrooms, thinly sliced

½ cup (120g) sauerkraut (with some brine tagging along)

3 ounces (85g) aged gouda, grated

fried toast with sugared tomatoes, burrata & chiles

Maybe, probably, definitely the easiest way to show off summer fruit? Toss it with sugar and let it be. Much like salt with vegetables, sugar makes fruit taste *fruitier*—juicy, syrupy, more like itself. Odds are you've done this with strawberries to pile on shortcakes or peaches to pair with cream. But what about tomatoes? Though technically a fruit, tomatoes often find themselves at lunch or dinner instead of dessert—and this recipe is no different. There is olive oil–crisped toast, a milky-melty orb of burrata, and just enough chile to make you do a double take. But instead of being simply salted, the tomatoes are sugared, too. Which means, even if you start with something bruised or mealy, you'll end up thinking you're eating the best tomato ever. And who's to say you're not?

SERVES 4

4 large ripe
heirloom tomatoes

2 tablespoons
granulated sugar,
plus more to taste

½ teaspoon kosher salt

½ teaspoon red
pepper flakes, plus
more for topping

Extra-virgin olive oil

8 thick slices bread

8 ounces (225g) burrata

Flaky salt (optional)

Roughly chop the tomatoes. Add to a bowl with the sugar, salt, and pepper flakes and gently stir to combine. Taste and increase the sugar as needed, depending on the tomatoes' ripeness.

Set a large cast-iron skillet over medium heat and add enough oil to thickly coat the bottom. When the oil is hot, add as many bread slices as will comfortably fit and pan-fry for 2 to 4 minutes per side, until deeply golden brown. Repeat with the remaining bread, adding more oil whenever the pan looks dry.

When all the toast is ready, divide among four plates or set on a platter. Spoon the tomatoes and their syrupy juices on top. Nestle a hunk of burrata amid the tomatoes. Drizzle with more oil and sprinkle with pepper flakes and flaky salt if you've got it. Don't try to pick these up—a fork and steak knife are your best bet.

fusilli with broccoli-cheddar sauce

Maybe you've seen (even made! and loved!) kale-sauced pasta. Ruth Rogers, Joshua McFadden, and Jamie Oliver all have their own takes, though the idea is similar: mostly Tuscan kale, boiled until tender, blended with garlic, olive oil, and cheese.

You can swap in other leafy things, like spinach or collards, or you can swap in other *green* things, like broccoli. To make an already little recipe even littler, I ditched the garlic. And instead of Parmesan or ricotta: melty cheddar. This yields such a fondue-like creaminess that the olive oil becomes unnecessary, too.

The most important ingredient is water. Obviously you need this to turn broccoli puree into broccoli sauce—and you could turn on the faucet and that would work fine. But since we're already boiling broccoli and pasta in water, why not use that seasoned, starchy stock? This not only thickens the sauce, it bumps up the green flavor, too.

Fill a stockpot with water and set over high heat to come to a boil.

When the water reaches a boil, generously season it with salt. Add the broccoli and cook for about 8 minutes, until it's bright green with tender-ish stalks. Use tongs or a spider to transfer the broccoli to a blender.

Return the water back to a boil and add the pasta. Set a timer for 8 minutes. After 2 to 3 minutes, once the pasta has released some of its starch, scoop out ⅔ cup (160ml) of the pasta water and add it to the blender along with the cheddar. Leave the keyhole in the blender lid open, cover with a kitchen towel and firm grip, and blend until smooth. Taste and add more cheese or salt if you want.

When the pasta timer goes off, try a noodle; it should be between toothsome and tender—keep cooking if it's not. Use a spider to transfer the pasta to a serving bowl (and don't drain that water). Add the broccoli-cheddar sauce to the pasta and toss. Add small splashes of broccoli-pasta water until the sauce reaches a thickness you like (keep in mind, it will thicken as it sits). Taste again and salt if needed. Serve with more cheddar for everyone to sprinkle on top.

SERVES 4

Kosher salt

1¼ pounds (570g) broccoli, florets and stalks roughly chopped

1 pound (455g) fusilli

2 ounces (55g) sharp white cheddar, grated, plus more for serving

rye puff pancake with greens & eggs

The puff pancake—also goes by German pancake, Bismarck pancake, and Dutch baby (but why?)—is a peak weekend breakfast or weekday breakfast-for-dinner. Think less American pancakes, which are halfway to cake, more oversized popover or Yorkshire pudding: eggy, crusty, and Grand Canyon–shaped. It's also mostly hands-off. Really, this is my favorite thing about puff pancakes—you can whisk up the batter in a matter of minutes, pour it into a blistering skillet, and let the oven take care of the rest. While that bakes, work on whatever toppings you want. My go-to is sautéed kale, sunny eggs, and crème fraîche (not in the least because the eggs and crème fraîche are already in the pancake). But don't let that stop you from swapping in another green (say, chard or spinach), or replacing it altogether with smoked salmon or bacon or prosciutto.

SERVES 2

puff pancake

3 large eggs

¼ cup (60g) crème fraîche

½ cup (65g) rye flour

½ teaspoon kosher salt

¼ teaspoon freshly ground black pepper

2 tablespoons unsalted butter

fixings

1 tablespoon unsalted butter

1 bunch Tuscan kale, stems removed, leaves chopped

Kosher salt and freshly ground black pepper

2 large eggs

Crème fraîche

Turn on the oven to 450°F (230°C) and immediately stick a 9-inch (23cm) or 10-inch (25cm) cast-iron skillet inside. Now work on the pancake batter. Combine the eggs, crème fraîche, and ⅓ cup (80ml) water in a bowl and whisk until smooth. Add the flour, salt, and pepper and whisk again.

Use oven mitts to transfer the skillet to the stove over medium heat. Add the butter, swirling the pan for full coverage. Once the butter has melted, whisk the batter, then pour it into the pan. Turn off the stove and get the skillet into the oven. Bake for 20 to 25 minutes, until the pancake has dramatically puffed.

While the pancake is baking, work on the greens. Melt ½ tablespoon of the butter in a large nonstick skillet over medium heat until it just starts to brown, then add the kale and toss a couple of times. Cover the pan and cook for 1 minute, until wilted. Uncover, sprinkle with salt and pepper, and cook for another 3 minutes or so, tossing occasionally, until tender. Taste and adjust the seasoning as needed, then transfer the greens to a bowl and lower the heat to medium-low.

Add the remaining ½ tablespoon butter to the emptied skillet. Once that's melted, crack in the eggs, sprinkle with salt and pepper, and cover the skillet. Cook for 2 to 3 minutes, checking frequently, until the whites are set but the yolks are still runny. Turn off the heat, uncover the skillet, and let the eggs hang out until the puff pancake is ready.

Serve the hot puff pancake with the greens, eggs, and spoonfuls of crème fraîche: You can arrange everything in the cast-iron skillet, or cut the pancake into pieces, transfer to two plates, and divvy up the toppings there.

tomato butter

MAKES ABOUT 2 CUPS (400G)

1 pint (320g) grape or cherry
tomatoes

¾ cup (170g) unsalted butter,
at room temperature

1½ teaspoons kosher salt

Halve each tomato. Now squeeze
out the pulp—either by pinching
the tomato, scooping with your
fingertip, or both. Add the seed-
less, juiceless tomatoes to a food
processor. Blitz until minced. Add
the butter and salt. Blend, scraping
down the sides every so often,
until the mixture is fluffy, homog-
enous, and rosy orange. At first,
it might seem as if it won't come
together, but it will. Use immediately, refrigerate for up to 5 days,
or freeze for up to 1 month.

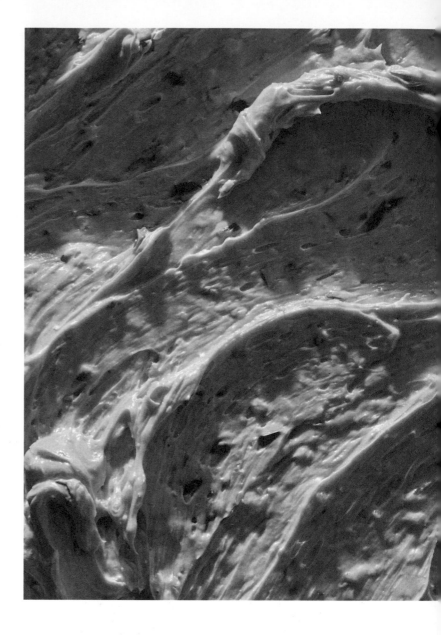

what to do in the winter

When tomatoes aren't feeling their best, lots of other ingredients are
happy to swoop in—especially wrinkly olives. Combine ½ cup (115g) of
soft unsalted butter with ½ cup (80g) of pitted oil-cured olives in a food
processor and blend, scraping down as needed, until fluffy and cocoa-
colored. Toss this butter with 1 pound (455g) of pasta cooked in shyly
salted boiling water (since the olives are salty). Serve with more olives
(pitted and torn into pieces) sprinkled on top. Ground Parmesan and/or
red pepper flakes are nice, too, if you have either around.

penne with tomato butter & buttered tomatoes

Arguably the internet's favorite tomato sauce comes by way of Italian cookbook author Marcella Hazan, who shared many tomato sauces over her lifetime. But the simplest one, with just onion and butter added, outshines them all. Such was the guiding light for this two-ingredient, no-cook pasta sauce, which, if you want to get nitty-gritty about it, is actually a compound butter. Classic no-cook sauce involves chopped tomatoes, olive oil, garlic, and basil. The catch, of course, is if your fork misses a tomato piece, you might as well be eating aglio e olio. So how do we guarantee tomatoey goodness in every bite like the cooked version? Puree instead of chop. When deseeded and blitzed with soft butter, tomatoes turn into rosy-cheeked fluff, which melts into sauce at the mention of hot pasta. Tomato butter also can and should be stirred into warm quinoa or rice, used as the starting point for sautéed zucchini or corn, or plunked on top of grilled chicken or swordfish.

Set a large pot of water over high heat to come to a boil.

While that's heating up, set a large skillet over medium-high heat and add ¼ cup (50g) of the tomato butter. As soon as it's melted, add the tomatoes. Cook, stirring often, until the tomatoes are jammy, deflated, and browning here and there, about 10 minutes. Turn off the heat.

When the water reaches a boil, generously season it with salt. Add the pasta and cook for 8 to 12 minutes, until al dente.

Reserve a mug-full of the pasta water, then drain the pasta. Add the pasta to the skillet with the tomatoes, along with the remaining ½ cup (100g) tomato butter. Toss and take a bite. Add pasta water, salt, and/or tomato butter if needed.

SERVES 4

¾ cup (150g) Tomato Butter (see recipe opposite), plus more to taste

2 pints (640g) grape or cherry tomatoes

Kosher salt

1 pound (455g) penne

meats & fishes

never underestimate schmaltz

Gravy is too much work for a weeknight, which is why I prefer this pan sauce that's practically a vinaigrette (or vinaigrette that's practically a pan sauce?). Next time you roast a chicken, scrape all the schmaltzy pan juices, including those bits stuck to the bottom, into a measuring cup. Estimate two parts pan juices to one part lemon juice or vinegar. Season with salt, stir with a fork, taste, and adjust the acid and salt until you'd drink it. This is just as good for chicken-dunking as it is for bread-sopping and lettuce-dressing.

skillet chicken thighs with schmaltzy, vinegary radishes

Add chicken thighs to a warmish skillet, let them take their time, and your patience will be rewarded with meat that's never dry, skin that's crunchier than a potato chip, and—if you ask me, this is the best part—lots of golden schmaltz. You could pour this into a jar and tuck it in the fridge for later. Or add vegetables right to the skillet for an all-in-one meal. Take radishes: Though these are often raw in salads, they love to be sautéed, becoming buttery tender and earthy sweet. Like beets and carrots, radishes are one ingredient that's actually two ingredients, thanks to those leafy greens you may or may not have been throwing out. To balance all the richness, an immodest amount of vinegar comes in at the end. You want something with plenty of brightness and contrast (like white wine vinegar), just not so much personality that it distracts from the rest of the dish (like balsamic). This dish can be seamlessly scaled up to serve four; just double the quantities and use two skillets instead.

Set a large cast-iron or nonstick skillet over medium heat. Pat-dry the chicken thighs and sprinkle all over with salt and pepper. Add the thighs, skin-side down, to the skillet. Cook for 15 to 25 minutes, adjusting the heat as needed so the skin doesn't brown too fast, until it's deeply golden brown and crispy.

While the chicken is cooking, use a knife to lop the greens off the radishes. Wash and dry the greens and set aside. Wash and dry the radishes, then halve them lengthwise (or quarter if they're large).

After you flip the chicken, set a timer for 5 minutes. When that goes off, push the chicken to the perimeter and add the radishes. Sprinkle with salt and toss radishes in the fat. Cook for another 15 minutes, until the radishes are tender and starting to brown, and the chicken is cooked through (165°F/75°C, though a little higher is fine; thighs are resilient).

Transfer the chicken to a plate. Add the radish greens to the pan and toss until they start to wilt, 1 minute or less. Turn off the heat, then stir in the vinegar. Nestle the chicken on top.

SERVES 2

4 bone-in, skin-on chicken thighs (about 1 pound/455g total)

Kosher salt and freshly ground black pepper

2 bunches radishes, leaves still attached

2 tablespoons (60ml) vinegar (white wine, rice, or apple cider)

braised brisket with forty cloves of garlic

While my mom's brisket recipe has a dozen ingredients, my own has become more to the point over the years. Just carrots, onions, and a *lot* of garlic—somewhere between five to twenty-five times as much as similar recipes. This is inspired by the Provençal classic, chicken with forty cloves of garlic. Thanks to such abundance, we can skip the traditional braising liquids like wine, beer, and broth. Because when the water simmers in the oven, it turns into broth. And when you reduce that broth on the stove, it turns into gravy so flavorful and bold and confident, it would put a chicken to shame. (For bonus zing, stir in prepared horseradish or red wine vinegar to taste.)

SERVES 6 TO 8

4 pounds (1.8kg) brisket

Kosher salt and freshly ground black pepper

2 tablespoons neutral oil

1¾ pounds (800g) carrots, peeled and chopped into big chunks

1½ pounds (685g) yellow onions, chopped into big chunks

40 garlic cloves, peeled (see tip opposite)

Set the brisket in a baking dish and massage all over with 4 teaspoons salt and a sprinkle of pepper. Cover and refrigerate for 12 hours to 2 days.

When you're ready to braise, heat the oven to 325°F (165°C). Set a large Dutch oven over medium-high heat and turn on the hood fan. While that heats up, pat-dry the brisket. (This helps it brown.) Add the oil to the pan and, when it's very hot, add the brisket. Sear until deeply browned all over, including the edges. Transfer to a plate.

Lower the heat to medium-low and add the carrots, onions, garlic, 1½ teaspoons salt, and a couple big pinches of pepper. Sauté, stirring occasionally, for a couple minutes.

Nestle the brisket on top of the vegetables, fatty-side up. Pour 3 to 4 cups (720 to 950ml) water around the perimeter until the water comes halfway up the meat. Increase the heat to bring the liquid to a simmer, cover the Dutch oven, and get it in the oven. Roast for 3 to 4 hours, until the brisket is fork-tender.

Raise the oven temperature to 350°F (175°C), uncover the Dutch oven, and cook for another 30 minutes, until the the top of the brisket is crusty. Carefully remove the pot from the oven. Transfer the brisket to a carving board. Use a slotted spoon to transfer the vegetables to a platter and sprinkle with salt and pepper. Tent both with aluminum foil.

Set the Dutch oven, now with only the braising liquid in it, over medium-high heat and boil until it's as reduced as you want. Season with salt and pepper to taste.

Slice the brisket against the grain, sprinkle with salt and pepper, and transfer to the platter with the vegetables. Serve with the gravy.

how to peel forty cloves of garlic without losing your mind

Choose your own hack: Lightly smoosh each clove with the side of a knife, then dump them in a bowl of warm water and peel there. Or, as an old coworker used to do, add the unpeeled cloves to a tightly lidded container and shake the living daylights out of it until the cloves spring out of their skins. (In a pinch, you can opt for pre-peeled cloves, though their flavor is less outspoken.)

bbq sauce

MAKES ¾ CUP (205G)

½ cup (135g) ketchup

¼ cup (60ml) apple cider vinegar

2 canned or jarred chipotle chiles en adobo, plus their sauce to taste

Kosher salt

Combine the ketchup, vinegar, and chipotles in a food processor or blender and buzz until completely smooth. Add adobo sauce and salt to taste. Store in the fridge for up to 1 week.

big beans love bbq sauce, too

For a vegetarian alternative (or just another good meal), ditch the pork and cook 12 ounces of dried gigantes, coronas, or big lima beans following the method used for the cannellini on page 55. The cooking time will vary by age and likely take longer due to their size. Once the beans are tender, strain, and toss with neutral oil or melted butter to taste. Top with ½ cup (135g) of the BBQ sauce, or more if you'd like.

pulled pork sandwiches with bbq sauce

BBQ sauce is not any one thing. In the United States, there's a Brady Bunch of regional styles, from Eastern North Carolina (vinegary as all get-out) to Alabama (uniquely mayo-based). But there is an overarching *idea* of BBQ sauce—tomatoey, peppery, molassesey—like the kind slathered on ribs at Chili's or shelved in stout bottles at the supermarket. The version in this recipe gets there with three ingredients: ketchup, apple cider vinegar, and chipotles en adobo (smoked, dried jalapeños rehydrated in a tingly tomato sauce). Blitzed together until smooth, these overachievers cover all of your sweet-tangy-smoky-spicy bases. The mixture stays uncooked, too, so its brightness can pep up falling-apart pork for sandwiches. The yield depends on how you distribute the meat; buoying it with shredded cabbage or sweet pickles will take it even further.

Season the pork all over with the salt. Transfer to a baking dish, cover, and refrigerate for 4 to 24 hours. (If you're pressed for time, skip the fridge and leave the salted pork on the counter for 45 minutes instead.)

When you're ready to cook, position a rack in the lower third of the oven and heat to 325°F (165°C).

Pat-dry the pork. (This helps it brown.) Set a large Dutch oven over high heat and add the oil. When the oil is very hot, add the pork. Sear on all sides, including the ends, until the crust is deeply browned all over. Turn off the heat.

Slowly add 1 cup (240ml) water to the pot. Cover the pot, stick it in the oven, and cook for 2½ to 3 hours, until the pork is fork-tender and falling apart.

If the pork was tied, remove and discard the butcher's twine. Use forks to shred the meat into big hunks right in the Dutch oven. Pour in ½ cup (135g) of the BBQ sauce and toss, adding more sauce to taste.

To build the sandwiches, pile meat on a slice of bread, top with more BBQ sauce, then close up with another slice of bread. If you have any leftover pork, store it in the fridge for up to 4 days.

MAKES 6 TO 10 SANDWICHES

2½ pounds (1.1kg) boneless pork butt

2½ teaspoons kosher salt

1 tablespoon neutral oil

BBQ Sauce (see recipe opposite)

12 to 20 slices bread (potato buns, warm tortillas, and cornbread slabs all work, too)

shrimp, walnuts & green onions in white wine

Can a recipe call for too many green onions? I don't think so. Also known as scallions, this member of the allium family is available all year long, with a flavor somewhere between onions and leeks. They're spicy and crunchy when raw, sweet and jammy when cooked. In this winey, walnutty, scampi-ish shrimp dish, they're treated both as an aromatic like garlic and as a green like kale. So, no, the three bunches for four people isn't a typo. Lean into it. I like to carry this sizzling skillet right to the table, set it alongside a loaf of bread (ciabatta is nice; warm is even nicer), and let everyone go at it. Dunking bread in the sauce isn't neat, but that's the whole point.

SERVES 4

3 bunches
green onions

¼ cup (55g)
unsalted butter

4 ounces (115g)
walnut halves (1 cup)

Kosher salt

¼ teaspoon red
pepper flakes, plus
more to taste

1¼ cups (300ml)
dry white wine

1 pound (455g) peeled
tail-on extra-large
shrimp, deveined

Remove the hairy bottoms from the green onions, then divide them into two even groups. Roughly chop one group into 1-inch (2.5cm) pieces, mince the other like garlic (green and white parts for both).

Set the largest skillet you've got over medium-low heat and add 1 tablespoon of the butter. When the butter has melted, add the walnuts and a pinch of salt. Cook, tossing frequently and lowering the heat if they're browning too quickly, for about 4 minutes, until the nuts are golden and fragrant. Transfer the nuts to a bowl but leave the heat on.

Add 1 tablespoon of the butter to the pan, along with the roughly chopped green onions and another pinch of salt. Cook over medium, stirring often, until the green onions are soft and starting to brown in some spots, about 3 minutes. Add another 1 tablespoon of the butter to the pan, followed by the minced green onions and red pepper flakes. Cook for another 3 minutes, until soft.

Stir in the wine and a pinch of salt. Bring to a simmer and cook for 1 minute. Add the shrimp, another pinch of salt, and the remaining 1 tablespoon butter. Cook for 2 to 4 minutes, until the shrimp just turn pink. Season the sauce with salt to taste. Sprinkle the walnuts on top, and add more red pepper flakes if you want.

lamb meatballs with zucchini & basil yogurt

Meatballs are often an everything-but-the-kitchen-sink situation, yet these call for only two things: ground lamb and more bread crumbs than you'd think. Rejiggering the usual ratio (lots of meat, little of everything else) stretches the most expensive ingredient and upgrades the texture. Fresh bread crumbs yield a tender interior and crostini-like crust. And while beef is the default meatball meat in the United States (and can be used here in a pinch), kofta—of which there are innumerable renditions across the Middle East, North Africa, and Indian subcontinent—frequently feature lamb for its gamey, can't-be-beat richness. These are perfect with any vegetable and creamy, tangy sauce, but especially juicy zucchini and herby yogurt.

Add the zucchini to a bowl and season with ¾ teaspoon salt. Toss with your hands, then leave on the counter to hang out.

Add the yogurt, basil, and a big pinch of salt to a food processor. Blend until the mixture is smooth and pea green, scraping down the sides as needed. Taste and add salt if needed. Transfer to a bowl and stick it in the fridge.

Combine the bread crumbs, 1 teaspoon salt, and ¾ cup (175ml) room-temp water in a bowl (more on this trick on page 11). Add the lamb and mix with your hands until everything is evenly distributed. Form into 2 tablespoon–size meatballs. (You should get about 15.)

Set the biggest cast-iron skillet you've got over medium-high heat. Pour in enough oil to thickly coat the bottom. When the oil is hot, add the meatballs. Cook for 8 to 10 minutes total, turning as they brown (and lowering the heat if they're darkening too quickly), until they're deeply browned, crusty, and cooked through. (I like medium.)

While the meatballs are cooking, drain the salted zucchini in a colander and pat-dry. When the meatballs are done, transfer them to a wire rack or plate and add the zucchini to the pan. Stir-fry for 5 to 7 minutes, until some slices are browned and buttery tender and others are slightly greener and firmer. Use a slotted spoon or spider to transfer the zucchini to a shallow bowl where it can stew in its own juices.

Serve the meatballs, zucchini, yogurt, and extra basil each in their own dishes. This way, everyone can build their own plates: a sweeping base of yogurt, topped with meatballs and zucchini, and sprinkled with basil.

SERVES 4

3 large zucchini, sliced into thick coins

Kosher salt

1 cup (240g) whole-milk Greek yogurt

2 cups (40g) packed basil leaves, plus more for topping

2 cups (150g) packed fresh bread crumbs (page 120)

1 pound (455g) ground lamb

Extra-virgin olive oil

pork meatloaf with cabbage slaw

Meatloaf at its best has a glossy-glazed crust and never-dry center. One of my favorite combos: ground beef (classic Americana), fresh bread crumbs (less drying than dried), sautéed onions (savory! sweet!), ketchup (mixed in and as the glaze), and water (yes, water). The result seems almost too soupy to hold shape—and, in turn, resists overcooking at all costs. I kept the same template here but re-casted the actors. Instead of beef: pork. Instead of ketchup: mustard. And instead of onions: cabbage. This last switch is—no offense to the others—the most exciting. Because when you invest in cabbage, you get twice the return. Half a head gets sautéed, deglazed with water, then mixed into the meatloaf. The other half becomes a mustardy slaw. I swiped this trick from another Food52 cookbook—*Dynamite Chicken* by Tyler Kord—so thanks, Tyler! Let's have a meatloaf party soon.

SERVES 6 TO 8

3 tablespoons
unsalted butter

1 medium head
green cabbage, cored
and thinly sliced

Kosher salt

2 whole-wheat
English muffins

3 large eggs

2 tablespoons
plus 1 teaspoon
Dijon mustard, plus
more for glazing

2 pounds (910g)
ground pork
(preferably
20 percent fat)

2 teaspoons extra-
virgin olive oil

Heat the oven to 350°F (175°C). Line a rimmed baking sheet with aluminum foil (for easier cleanup).

In a large skillet, melt the butter over medium heat, then add half of the cabbage. Stir in a big pinch of salt, then cover the pan. Cook for 5 minutes to wilt, then remove the lid and cook for about 10 minutes more, stirring occasionally, until the cabbage is very soft and caramelized in spots. Turn off the heat, add ¾ cup (175ml) water to the pan, and use a spoon to scrape up the browned bits stuck to the bottom. Remove the pan from the heat.

Tear each English muffin into chunks, add to a food processor, and pulse until very fine. In a large bowl, combine the English-muffin crumbs, eggs, the 2 tablespoons Dijon, and 1 tablespoon salt. Add the pork and mix with your hands until mostly combined, then mix in the cooled cabbage.

Dump the meatloaf mixture onto the baking sheet. Form into a loafish shape, roughly 12 by 4½ inches (30 by 11.5cm). Rub Dijon all over.

Bake for 45 to 60 minutes, rotating the pan halfway through, until firm to the touch and the internal temperature is 155°F to 160°F (65°C to 70°C). Remove from the oven and let rest for about 15 minutes before slicing.

Add the remaining cabbage to a bowl and sprinkle with salt. Massage the cabbage and let it hang out for 10 minutes. Add the oil and the 1 teaspoon Dijon, toss, and adjust the salt to taste. Serve the meatloaf slices with a pile of slaw.

on oil-packed tuna, which turns everything it touches into gold

On a good week, my pantry is full of canned tuna. Not because I have a specific dinner lined up or because I regularly take sandwiches for lunch or because my cat enjoys it (actually, it upsets her stomach), but because tuna is the ultimate sidekick. When you forget to buy groceries or find that whatever you were planning to eat has crossed over to the other side, tuna is there. Tuna is ready. Tuna has your back. This humble ingredient is cost-effective, shelf-stable, ready-to-eat, and full of umami. Try to find a brand that fishes sustainably, be it pole-and-line or trolling. Though I grew up in a water-packed tuna family, these days I'm oil-packed all the way. The fish is butterier in texture, richer in flavor, and happier in finished dishes—like these five—all of which use one can of tuna plus four or fewer other ingredients.

broccoli salad with garlicky beans & tuna
SERVES 2 TO 4

Trim the bottoms of 1¼ pounds (570g, 2 medium or 3 small) broccoli heads, then peel away the outer layer of the stalks. Slice the stalks into thin-as-possible coins, chop the tops into tiny-as-can-be florets, and toss with ½ teaspoon kosher salt in a bowl. Pour ¼ cup (60ml) extra-virgin olive oil into a nonstick skillet over medium heat. When that's hot, add 6 to 8 chopped garlic cloves. Stir-fry until the garlic starts to turn golden, then add 1 drained, rinsed, and dried (15-ounce/425g) can cannellini beans and a pinch of salt. Cook for a couple of minutes, until the beans start to crisp, then stir in 1 drained (5-ounce/140g) can oil-packed tuna and drop the heat to low. While the tuna warms up, toss the broccoli with olive oil and freshly squeezed lemon juice to taste, then transfer to a platter. Top the broccoli with the beans and tuna and serve with lemon wedges.

tuna artichoke melt

MAKES 4 SLICES

Broil 4 slices of bread on a baking sheet until both sides are deeply golden brown. Drain 1 (12-ounce/340g) jar marinated artichokes (reserve the marinade), then roughly chop. Add to a bowl with 1 drained (5-ounce/140g) can oil-packed tuna. Mash with a fork, adding artichoke marinade as needed until it's like tuna salad. Divide among the toasts, then top with sharp cheddar (1 to 2 slices per piece). Broil until the cheese is melty and blistering.

avocado toast with tuna

MAKES 2 SLICES

Toast 2 slices of bread however you want (toaster, broiler, pan). Halve, pit, and peel 1 small ripe avocado and add to a bowl with 1 drained (5-ounce/140g) can oil-packed tuna, 1 tablespoon freshly squeezed lemon juice, and a big pinch each of kosher salt and freshly ground black pepper. Mash with a fork until it's as smooth or chunky as you want, adjust the seasonings to taste, then divide between the toast. Finish with another squeeze of lemon and a sprinkle of salt and pepper. (Psst: If you want a more avocado-y situation, you can use a large avocado, then stretch to 3 to 4 slices.)

tuna pasta with green olives & nori

SERVES 2

Set a large pot of water over high heat. Once boiling, generously season it with salt and add 8 ounces (225g) penne or another short-shape pasta and cook until al dente. Combine 1 drained (5-ounce/140g) can oil-packed tuna, ⅓ cup (50g) pitted, halved Castelvetrano olives, and 3 tablespoons extra-virgin olive oil in a big bowl. Use a spider to transfer the pasta to the bowl, toss, and season with pasta water, salt, and/or olive oil to taste (also red pepper flakes if you want). Crumble 1 (0.17-ounce/5g) pack of salted, roasted seaweed on top.

potatoes with tonnato & arugula

SERVES 4 TO 6

Set a large pot of water over high heat to come to a boil. Halve 2 pounds (910g) baby yellow potatoes. Combine 1 drained (5-ounce/140g) can oil-packed tuna, ⅓ cup (80g) mayonnaise, 3 tablespoons white wine vinegar, and a pinch each of kosher salt and freshly ground black pepper in a food processor. Blend, scraping down the sides as needed, until smooth. Adjust the seasoning to taste. Boil the potatoes until they're knife-tender (start checking after 8 minutes), then use a spider to transfer them to a platter where they can stretch out in a single layer. Drizzle with white wine vinegar. Spoon the tuna-mayo in a Jackson Pollock–ish pattern on top and scatter with a couple huge handfuls of baby arugula.

rib-eye with sizzled capers & humongous parsley salad

Roasted marrow bones and parsley salad: Though St. John, the restaurant that made this dish famous, is in London, the first place I ever tried it was Raleigh, North Carolina, at a little restaurant called Stanbury, where I ended up getting married. There are capers and shallots, flaky salt and napkins. It is restaurant food. But also dirty-martini food, date-night food, just-us food.

This is how I make it at home. Instead of marrow bones, a reverse-seared rib-eye is just as meaty and fatty and good. But the capers are the hero. Some get blitzed with salt for an ultra-briny dry-brine (this takes a couple of hours at least, so plan ahead). Others get crisped alongside the steak. The vinegar from the jar goes on to quick-pickle shallots. And that shallot-infused vinegar goes on to dress parsley. Some might say that something so allium-y is unromantic, but there's nothing less romantic to me than someone who doesn't like alliums.

Combine ⅓ cup (55g) capers and 1¼ teaspoons salt in a food processor and mince. Pat-dry the rib-eye and rub it all over with the caper-salt. Transfer to a container or ziplock bag and refrigerate for 2 hours to 2 days.

When you're ready to cook, remove the steak from the fridge and heat the oven to 275°F (135°C). Add the shallots to a big bowl, cover with 3 tablespoons caper brine, and stir. Transfer the steak to a baking sheet and roast, flipping halfway through, for 25 to 40 minutes, until an instant-read thermometer inserted in the center registers 115°F/46°C (medium-rare) to 125°F/52°C (medium).

Pluck the parsley leaves from the stems, then wash and dry both separately. Mince the stems, like you would chives. Leave the leaves as they are or roughly chop.

Once the steak is out of the oven, set a cast-iron skillet over medium-high heat for a few minutes, until it's starting to smoke. Use a butter knife to scrape the caper brine from the steak, then pat-dry. Add enough oil to the skillet to thinly coat the bottom, then add the steak and sprinkle the remaining 2 tablespoons capers around the perimeter. Cook the steak for 1 to 2 minutes per side, until deeply browned. (If the capers start to burn, remove them earlier.)

Add the prepped parsley to the pickled shallots, along with 2 tablespoons oil, and toss. Taste and adjust the caper brine and oil if needed.

Serve the steak with the crispy capers on top and the salad alongside.

SERVES 2

⅓ cup plus
2 tablespoons (75g)
drained capers,
brine reserved

Kosher salt

1¼ pounds (570g)
bone-in rib-eye

2 shallots, thinly sliced

2 bunches flat-leaf
parsley

Extra-virgin olive oil

slow-roasted halibut with harissa beans & yogurty cucumbers

In most scenarios—say, in a skillet, under the broiler, on the grill—it's all too easy to overcook fish. But in a barely warm oven (a Genius method I learned from Sally Schneider), you could forget to set a timer and still come out ahead. This works wonders with just about any seafood you can get your hands on, be it halibut, swordfish, salmon, tuna, bass, cod, or scallops.

Here, halibut slow-roasts atop white beans, sauced with harissa and more olive oil than you'd think. A high-impact North African ingredient, harissa is a chile paste with myriad spices (like cumin, caraway, and coriander, though the specifics vary widely). You can purchase it as a concentrated paste in a tube or looser sauce in a jar, but this recipe uses the former. (If you can only find the latter, avoid anything that calls itself mild, and increase the quantity to taste.) In lieu of English cucumbers, you can swap in another variety—just remove any noticeable seeds.

SERVES 4

¾ cup (175ml) extra-virgin olive oil

2 tablespoons harissa, plus more to taste

Kosher salt

2 (15-ounce/425g) cans cannellini beans, drained (not rinsed)

1¼ pounds (565g) halibut (or another white fish), skin removed

2 English cucumbers

1 cup (240g) whole-milk Greek yogurt

Heat the oven to 275°F (135°C). Add the oil, harissa, and a pinch of salt to a 2-quart (1.9L) or similar baking dish and stir. Taste and increase the harissa if needed. Gently stir in the beans. Season the fish all over with salt, then nestle amid the beans. Roast for 25 to 40 minutes (depending on the size of the fillets), until the fish reaches 120°F (50°C) in the middle and flakes at the touch of a fork.

While that's roasting, smack the cucumbers with the side of a chef's knife or rolling pin until they split like a dropped watermelon. Now roughly chop them. Add to a bowl with a few pinches of salt and stir.

Once the fish is out of the oven, pour the salted cucumbers into a colander or sieve to drain their juices. Evenly swoosh the yogurt between four plates, then sprinkle the cucumbers on top of each.

Serve the warm fish and beans alongside the cucumber salad, with spicy oil to spoon on top.

pork tenderloin with buttery kimchi & apples

While pork shoulder can stay in the oven for an hour longer than intended and still be delicious (honestly maybe even better), pork tenderloin goes from just-right to chalky in minutes. Brining is an easy way to avoid this. Salt water works, but there's nothing stopping you from swapping in feta liquid or pickle juice or, in this case, kimchi brine. This foundational, fermented Korean ingredient manifests in many forms, but the best-known is baechu kimchi, which hinges on Napa cabbage. Here, that gets sautéed, then roasted alongside pork, a classic companion to kimchi, with a couple of chopped apples for welcome sweetness. Adding more brine to the skillet yields a fuss-free sauce, ready to be spooned over polenta, quinoa, or rice.

Add ⅔ cup (160ml) water, ⅓ cup (80ml) kimchi brine, and the salt to a bowl or container and stir. Add the pork and make sure it's submerged, adding more water and/or kimchi brine if needed. Cover and refrigerate for 2 to 12 hours.

When the pork is done brining, remove it from the liquid and pat-dry. Heat the oven to 400°F (200°C).

Set a large cast-iron skillet over medium-high heat. When the pan is hot, add the oil and swirl it around. Add the pork—if you have to curve it to fit, that's okay. Brown it on all sides, about 6 minutes total. Add the kimchi and apples, evenly distributing on either side of the pork. Pour ⅓ cup (80ml) kimchi brine on top of the kimchi and apples, then sprinkle with the butter pieces. Get the skillet in the oven.

Roast for 12 to 15 minutes, flipping the pork halfway through and stirring the kimchi and apples so everything cooks evenly, until the middle of the pork registers 140°F to 145°F/60°C to 63°C (a little pink in the center is good—that means it's not dried out).

When the pork is done, let it rest in the skillet for a few minutes, then transfer it to a carving board and slice. Nestle the slices on top of the kimchi and apples.

SERVES 2 TO 4

1⅓ cups (215g) roughly chopped kimchi, brine reserved

2 teaspoons kosher salt

1 to 1½ pounds (455 to 685g) pork tenderloin

1½ tablespoons neutral oil

2 medium apples (such as Honeycrisp or Jonagold), cored and cut into chunks

2 tablespoons unsalted butter, chopped

sesame chicken with artichokes & arugula

This is not sesame chicken. Well, not like that. The American-Chinese takeout dish was my muse, but by rejiggering those namesake flavors—sesame seeds and chicken and that's it—you can cook up something that closer resembles a chicken cutlet. Known around the world by many names—like German schnitzel, Italian Milanese, Mexican milanesa, Japanese katsu—this is where the meat is pounded thin, tumbled in crumbs, and pan-fried until crisp.

    This recipe celebrates that sort of minimalism. After being bashed around in a mortar, sesame seeds turn into a highly nutty, super crunchy, not-bread breading. When it comes to the chicken, breasts are easier to pound but also easier to overcook, while thighs are wonkier-shaped but juicier. You could make the accompanying salad in your sleep: drained marinated artichokes and a confident lettuce (like arugula, radicchio, or endive), plus a splash of artichoke marinade as a no-effort dressing if you want it. I want it.

SERVES 2

½ cup (70g) white
sesame seeds

Kosher salt

2 boneless, skinless
chicken breasts or
4 boneless, skinless
chicken thighs (about
1 pound/455g total)

Neutral oil

1 (12-ounce/340g)
jar quartered and
marinated artichokes,
drained, marinade
reserved

4 cups (80g)
baby arugula

Add the sesame seeds to a mortar and roughly crush with the pestle until some seeds are powdery and others whole. (A mini food processor or spice grinder also works.) Stir in ¾ teaspoon salt, then dump the mixture onto a rimmed plate or pie pan.

If you're using chicken breasts, halve them horizontally. If you're using thighs, leave as is. Place the chicken between two pieces of parchment and, with a rolling pin or the bottom of a skillet, pound to an even ¼-inch (6mm) thickness. Dredge the pounded chicken in the sesame mixture, pressing firmly to coat.

Set a cast-iron skillet over medium-high heat and add enough oil to thinly coat the bottom. When a few sesame seeds dropped into the pan instantly sizzle, not sink to the bottom or burn, the pan is ready.

Add the sesame-coated chicken to the pan in a single layer—do this in batches if necessary so they brown, not steam. Cook for 2 to 4 minutes per side, until the outside is golden and the inside is cooked through (160°F/70°C for breasts and 165°F/75°C for thighs). Transfer to a cooling rack and sprinkle with salt. Repeat with any remaining chicken, adding more oil to the pan as needed.

While the last batch is cooking, combine the artichokes, arugula, and a pinch of salt in a big bowl. Toss and add artichoke marinade to taste.

Serve the sesame chicken while it's still hot, with the salad alongside.

another not-bread breading

After you master this recipe, swap out the sesame seeds for ⅓ cup (45g) poppy seeds. Equally crunchy, extra dramatic, and no need to bash in a mortar—just combine them with ¾ teaspoon salt on a rimmed plate or pie pan, and proceed to step two.

what about those chard stems?

Glad you asked! Keep in the fridge for tomorrow or the day after. When you're ready to eat, thinly slice the stems and set a large skillet over medium heat. Add enough olive oil to thinly coat the bottom and, when that's hot, add the stems, 1 or 2 minced garlic cloves, and a pinch of salt. Cook, stirring occasionally, until the stems are crisp-tender, 5 to 8 minutes. Turn off the heat and squeeze lemon juice on top, plus freshly ground black pepper or red pepper flakes to taste. This would be awesome next to roast chicken, fried eggs, takeout pizza, you name it.

apricot-mustard salmon with massaged chard

Along with mushroom puffs, anchovy-parsley dip, and eggplant spread, one of my family's go-to party starters is a colossal Hebrew National salami, scored, baked, and brushed with a two-ingredient glaze: equal parts apricot jam and Dijon mustard. Besides being easy enough for a child (that was me) to assemble, it's spicy, sweet, and finger-licking (also me) good when caramelized. So why should salami get to have all the fun? Turns out, this glaze is wonderful with any rich protein—especially salmon. If you can't track down rainbow or Swiss chard, kale can step in. This recipe seamlessly halves to serve two.

Use your hands to separate the chard's stems and leaves. Save the stems for another day (see tip opposite). Slice the leaves into thin ribbons and add to a large bowl. Sprinkle with salt and gently massage to slightly soften.

Position a rack in the upper quarter of the oven and turn on the broiler. Pat-dry the salmon, then sprinkle all over with salt. Combine the jam and Dijon in a small bowl and season with salt to taste.

Line a rimmed baking sheet with aluminum foil. Heat a large skillet over medium-high heat. Add 2 teaspoons oil and, when that's hot, add the salmon, skin-side down, and immediately press with a spatula (this prevents curling). Drop the heat to medium-low and cook for 4 minutes.

Meanwhile, drizzle the chard with oil and lemon juice to sight. Toss, taste, and adjust the salt, oil, and lemon juice if needed—aim for punchy-bright, since the salmon is rich.

After 4 minutes, turn off the stove, flip the salmon, and use the spatula (or your fingers) to peel off the skin. Lay the skin pieces across one half of the baking sheet. Flip the salmon again (so the barely cooked side is facing up), transfer to the empty half of the baking sheet, and brush the glaze on top. Broil for 3 to 4 minutes, checking frequently, until the glaze is bubbling and the skin is crisp as a cracker (you may need to rotate the pan to encourage even cooking or remove the skin earlier if it's ready first).

Serve the glazed salmon and chard salad with lemon wedges to squeeze and crispy salmon skin to crumble on top.

SERVES 4

2 bunches rainbow or Swiss chard

Extra-virgin olive oil

Kosher salt

4 (6-ounce/170g) skin-on salmon fillets

¼ cup (80g) apricot jam

¼ cup (60g) Dijon mustard

Freshly squeezed lemon juice, plus wedges for serving

vegetables that aren't sides

cream-braised fennel with anchovies

When you reach that point in winter when you just want it to be spring, make this. Like broccoli and carrots, fennel is supermarket-dependable year-round and, come those cloudy-gusty weeks when I'm wanting something—anything—green, it's ready to step in. Here, the bulbs are browned in anchovy oil, then braised in anchovy cream—which you are maybe thinking is a lot of anchovy in one sentence. But just how much is up to you. For anchovy novices, start with one tin and grow your romance with this briny-brawny fish from there. For anchovy lovers, double that. Or land somewhere in between. While the bulbs are in the oven, the stalks (never throw these out!) quick-pickle in salt and vinegar for a zingy-zesty topping. I like this best with a crusty sourdough for mopping up the sauce.

Heat the oven to 375°F (190°C). While that warms up, pluck a big handful of fennel fronds, wash and dry them, and set aside. With a knife or mandoline, very thinly slice enough fennel stalks to yield 1¼ cups (150g). Place the slices in a bowl, sprinkle with 1 teaspoon salt, and stir. Pour the vinegar on top and stir again.

Use a vegetable peeler to shave away any tough outer leaves, then halve the fennel bulbs lengthwise. (You can cut out the triangular cores or leave them be.) Set a large, ovenproof Dutch oven, cast-iron skillet, or sauté pan over medium heat. (You'll need a lid.) Add 2 tablespoons anchovy oil to the pan. When that's hot, add as many fennel bulbs as will fit, cut-side down. Cook until deeply browned on the bottom, 4 to 8 minutes. Transfer to a plate, then repeat with the remaining bulbs, adding more oil if the pan looks dry.

As the fennel sears, combine the minced anchovies, heavy cream, and black pepper in a bowl. As soon as the second batch of fennel bulbs is ready, flip them over, then return the rest of the fennel to the skillet, browned side facing up (it's okay if they overlap). Sprinkle each bulb with a few grains of salt, then pour the anchovy cream around the fennel. Bring to a simmer, then cover the pan and get it in the oven.

Bake for 30 minutes, then uncover and bake for another 15 to 25 minutes, until the fennel is knife-tender and the cream has thickened. (If the fennel finishes before the cream, transfer the fennel to a plate, then simmer the cream on the stove until it's as thick as you want.)

Sprinkle the fronds on top of the fennel and anchovy cream, and serve with the vinegary fennel pickles to spoon on top.

SERVES 4

4 large heads fennel, bulbs separated from stalks

Kosher salt

½ cup (120ml) white wine vinegar

1 to 2 (2-ounce/55g) tins oil-packed anchovy fillets (see headnote), fish minced and oil reserved

2 cups (480ml) heavy cream

1 teaspoon freshly ground black pepper

sweet potato skins with tempeh crumbles & chipotle yogurt

Even though I eat meat, my fridge's meat drawer (is this the technical term?) is rarely filled with beef, chicken, or pork. Instead, you'll find a cheese or two, maybe a container of boiled eggs, and always tempeh. Made from fermented soybeans and pressed into a dense, chewy cake, this Indonesian ingredient is equal parts hearty and nourishing, with a nutty flavor and sturdy shelf life. Because of its mushroom-like umami, it gets along great with other big-flavor ingredients like brown rice, whole-wheat noodles, or squashy sweet potatoes. Try to find spuds that are more oval than round in shape—all the better to turn into cheesy, yogurty, tempeh-stuffed boats. This recipe effortlessly halves to serve two.

SERVES 4

4 large sweet potatoes

Neutral oil

Kosher salt

2 (8-ounce/225g) packages tempeh

2 chipotle chiles en adobo, minced, sauce reserved

1 cup (240g) whole-milk Greek yogurt

4 ounces (115g) sharp cheddar, grated

⅔ cup (60g) finely chopped green onions

Heat the oven to 450°F (230°C). Scrub the sweet potatoes under water, then pat-dry. Add to a rimmed baking sheet, rub with oil, then sprinkle all over with salt. Roast for about 50 minutes, flipping halfway through, until fork-tender.

While the sweet potatoes roast, crumble the tempeh into a bowl in bite-size nuggets and season with 1 teaspoon oil, 2 teaspoons adobo sauce, and a pinch of salt. Toss until the tempeh is coated.

Add the yogurt to another bowl, along with the minced chipotles and a pinch of salt. Stir, taste, and add some adobo sauce if you'd like.

When the potatoes are done, carefully transfer them to a cutting board. Immediately add the tempeh to the hot baking sheet and bake for 5 to 7 minutes, until beginning to brown.

As the tempeh bakes, halve the sweet potatoes lengthwise. Use a spoon to scoop out most of the filling (reserve for another use, see tip opposite), leaving a ¼- to ½-inch (6mm to 1.3cm) border. After you pull the tempeh from the oven, place a rack in the upper quarter of the oven, and turn on the broiler.

Place the sweet potato skins on the baking sheet. Evenly divide the tempeh among the skins, then sprinkle the cheddar on top. Broil for about 3 minutes, checking regularly, until the cheese has melted and is starting to brown in spots. Sprinkle the green onions on top and serve with the chipotle yogurt.

smoky, spicy, yogurt mashed potatoes

So, you've got some sweet potato bellies, chipotle chiles en adobo sauce, and Greek yogurt in the fridge. Here's the plan for sometime this week: Warm up the sweet potato (microwave, stovetop, or a low-temp oven all work), then stir in ¼ cup (60g) yogurt, a minced chipotle, and a pinch of salt. Taste and adjust the creaminess and spiciness if needed. Drizzle with maple syrup or honey, and top with flaky salt. This is so nice with any protein, from chicken or pork to tofu or fish.

crunchy-shell cauliflower tacos

This is the first Big Little Recipe we ever published. It was 2018, when cauliflower rice was everywhere you looked. Maybe it's because I eat rice—like, actual rice—most days of the week, but I never found this trend to be very convincing. Because if I blitz up cauliflower into confetti, I don't want to turn it into rice. I want to turn it into ground beef. Tossed with oil and chili powder, then blasted in a hot oven, this once-meek vegetable gains loads of meaty confidence. The trick is to divide what could fit on one baking sheet between two so the cauliflower can crisp and caramelize as much as possible. Tucked into a taco shell (you can use soft corn or flour if you feel strongly about it) with shredded iceberg and grated cheese, I'd take this over beef any day. Add a shimmy of hot sauce if you'd like.

Heat the oven to 450°F (230°C) and get out two rimmed baking sheets.

Remove the bottom of the cauliflower stem, as well as the green leaves, and roughly chop the rest. Add one-third of the cauliflower florets to a food processor and pulse until they're almost riced—some chunks here and there are nice. Dump onto one baking sheet. Process the remaining cauliflower florets in two batches and add to the same baking sheet. Add the oil, chili powder, and ¾ teaspoon salt, and toss with your hands. Evenly divide this mixture between the two baking sheets.

Roast for 20 to 30 minutes, rotating the pans halfway through, until the cauliflower is browned and crisp. Taste and season with more salt if you want.

Add the taco shells to the oven—directly on a rack works fine—to toast for a couple of minutes, until warm.

Assemble the tacos in the following order: cauliflower, lettuce, cheese. Or go rogue.

MAKES 8 TACOS

1 large head cauliflower

3 tablespoons neutral oil

3½ teaspoons chili powder

Kosher salt

8 crunchy taco shells

1 cup (45g) shredded iceberg (about ¼ lettuce head)

1 cup (120g) grated pepper Jack cheese

sour cream & onion squash kugel

A cozy baked pudding slash casserole, Jewish kugel might start with potatoes or matzo, or, my family's favorite, egg noodles. In our recipe, as in many, these get combined with cottage cheese, eggs, sugar, and raisins, then topped with so many cornflakes. It is more sweet than savory, more dessert than dinner, even though it's served as a side. This is not that kugel. Because instead of noodles, there is spaghetti squash—mixed with roasted onions and sour cream, covered in crushed potato chips. It's as welcome at Shabbat as it would be at Thanksgiving. Or, pair it with a vinegary salad and call it dinner any time. For what it's worth, there's no graceful way to cut winter squash, but a meat cleaver is my weapon of choice.

SERVES 4 TO 6

1 large spaghetti squash, halved and seeded

2 medium yellow onions, thinly sliced

3 tablespoons extra-virgin olive oil

Kosher salt and freshly ground black pepper

1 cup (240g) sour cream

2 large eggs

3 cups (75g) potato chips

Heat the oven to 450°F (230°C). Add the squash to one baking sheet and the onions to another. Rub the squash with 2 tablespoons of the oil and sprinkle with salt and pepper. Add the remaining 1 tablespoon oil to the onions, sprinkle with salt and pepper, and toss. Put both sheets in the oven. Roast the onions for about 20 minutes, until soft and translucent with some slices starting to brown, and the squash for 35 to 45 minutes, until easily shreddable with a fork.

Meanwhile, combine the sour cream, eggs, ½ teaspoon salt, and ¼ teaspoon pepper in a large bowl, and whisk until smooth.

When the onions are done, let them cool for a few minutes, then stir them into the sour cream mixture. When the squash is done, lower the oven temperature to 375°F (190°C), then shred the squash with a fork onto a large plate to cool until warm.

Transfer a big handful of shredded squash to a tea towel and squeeze over a bowl to get rid of excess liquid, then stir the squash into the sour cream mixture. Repeat with the remaining squash. (This will yield a lot of liquid, up to a couple cups total. You can pour it down the drain, pretend it's vegetable stock in another recipe, or slurp it straight.)

Transfer the kugel mixture to a 2½-quart (2.4L) baking dish, spread it out, and crumble the potato chips on top. Bake for 20 to 30 minutes, until the kugel is set in the middle. (You can poke a paring knife in and take a peek.) Let cool for a few minutes before serving.

today's bread butts are tomorrow's bread crumbs

Bread ends are often seen as scraps, but scraps are worthy in
their own way. Thanks to the Maillard reaction (aka the browning
reaction), a loaf's crust boasts its biggest flavor, which is why
I never throw out those odds and ends: Instead, chop them into
bite-size pieces and collect them in an airtight container in the
freezer. Once it fills up, thaw the pieces at room temp, then pulse
in a food processor until fine. At this point, you can use the bread
crumbs right away or freeze them again for down the road.

open-faced eggplant parm

Usually eggplant Parm goes something like this: Make tomato sauce. Slice eggplants into rounds, season with salt, and let drain. Set up a dredging station with flour on one plate, eggs and milk on another, and cheesy bread crumbs on another. Dredge the eggplant slices, shallow-fry in batches, then layer the fried eggplant, tomato sauce, mozzarella, and Parmesan in a casserole dish. Bake until bubbly, cool for a bit, and serve. Great weeknight recipe, right?

But the thing is, it should be. That's why I opt to look at eggplant Parm less like lasagna, more like an open-faced sandwich (the best kind of sandwich). Each person gets a honking roasted eggplant half—doused in jammy tomato sauce (just canned tomatoes, olive oil, and salt), gobs of fresh mozzarella, and bread crumbs that toast while cheese becomes weak in the knees under the broiler. It's way more hands-off and just as good with red wine.

SERVES 4

1 (28-ounce/795g) can whole peeled tomatoes

3 tablespoons extra-virgin olive oil, plus more for drizzling

Kosher salt

2 large globe eggplants, halved lengthwise

8 ounces (225g) fresh mozzarella, thinly sliced

¼ cup (30g) ground or grated Parmesan

1 cup (75g) packed fresh bread crumbs (see tip opposite)

Combine the tomatoes and their juices, the oil, and 1 teaspoon salt in a large saucepan. Partially cover and set over medium heat to come to a boil. Cook, aiming for somewhere between a simmer and a boil, for 30 to 40 minutes, until thick and jammy; stir every so often, smooshing the tomatoes to help them break down. (You can make the sauce in advance, store for several days in the fridge, and rewarm before using.)

While the tomato sauce is cooking, heat the oven to 400°F (200°C). Cut a ½-inch (1.3cm) crosshatch pattern in the flat side of each eggplant half, like a duck breast. Place on a rimmed baking sheet, crosshatch-side up, and drizzle with oil and sprinkle with salt. Roast for 25 to 35 minutes, until tender.

Once the eggplant is done, place a rack in the upper quarter of the oven and turn on the broiler. Top each eggplant half with 6 tablespoons (90ml) tomato sauce. (You'll have about ½ cup/120ml left over for pasta or grilled cheese sandwiches later in the week.) Evenly divide the mozzarella slices and Parmesan on top, then sprinkle with the bread crumbs.

Broil, watching closely, for about 2 minutes, rotating the pan if needed, until the mozzarella is gooey and the bread crumbs are toasty.

no, veggie burgers don't need a billion ingredients

Or even a dozen. In fact, each burger here has only three, and no one will be the wiser. The trick is to start with soaked, not cooked, beans. Such is the time-tested strategy for Middle Eastern falafel—though I never thought to falafel-ify veggie burgers until I read Joe Yonan's wonderful cookbook *Cool Beans*. Unlike the canned sort, which hold together well but mush-out at first bite, rehydrated beans yield a crackly crust and meaty center. Though you can channel this toward all sorts of varieties (Joe's Genius Recipe uses black), I like flavor-seeking chickpeas best. So grab a squishy bun, and let's get started.

1.
soak it all in

For 5 or 6 burgers, soak 1 cup (180g) dried chickpeas in water for 12 to 24 hours. Drain, then add to a food processor with 1 teaspoon kosher salt. Pulse, scraping down the sides as needed, until the beans are finely minced and easily hold together when squeezed. Transfer the ground chickpeas to a bowl.

2.
pick your mix-ins

green olive + parsley

Add ½ bunch flat-leaf parsley, roughly chopped (stems included!) to the food processor and pulse a couple times. Add ⅔ cup (100g) halved Castelvetrano olives and pulse until minced. Add this mixture to the chickpeas and stir to combine.

artichoke + sun-dried tomato

Drain 1 (12-ounce/340g) can marinated artichokes and add to the food processor. Pulse until minced, then mix into the chickpeas. Add ½ cup (70g) drained, julienned sun-dried tomatoes to the food processor, pulse until minced, then mix into the chickpeas and artichokes.

poblano + pecan

Remove the stems and seeds from 1 pound poblanos, then roughly chop. Sauté in a slick of neutral oil with a couple pinches of kosher salt until charred and soft, 10 to 15 minutes over medium heat. Meanwhile, add 1½ cups (175g) raw pecan pieces to the food processor and pulse until they're halfway between pecan flour and pecan butter. Add to the chickpeas and mix. When the peppers are done, add them to the food processor and pulse until minced, then mix into the chickpeas and pecans.

3.
chill out

Use your hands to form the mixture into 5 or 6 burgers. Refrigerate them in an airtight container or on a covered plate for 1 hour to 1 week. This helps them hold their shape in the pan.

4.
now you're cooking

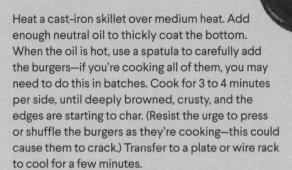

Heat a cast-iron skillet over medium heat. Add enough neutral oil to thickly coat the bottom. When the oil is hot, use a spatula to carefully add the burgers—if you're cooking all of them, you may need to do this in batches. Cook for 3 to 4 minutes per side, until deeply browned, crusty, and the edges are starting to char. (Resist the urge to press or shuffle the burgers as they're cooking—this could cause them to crack.) Transfer to a plate or wire rack to cool for a few minutes.

5.
let's eat

Grab a potato bun or English muffin or pita or some grainy toast. Now sandwich your burger with a couple toppings.

---

highly recommended combos

spicy mayo
+

onion slivers

---

pepper jack
+
juicy tomato

---

garlic mayo
+

baby arugula

---

dijon mustard
+
bread-and-butter pickles

jammy peppers with warm feta & crispy lentils

Caramelized onions get a lot of hype, but caramelized peppers might be even better. Technicolored, sweet as corn, and at-the-ready during any season, bell peppers long to be melted into oblivion—until they're tender, buttery, and halfway to jam. To turn these into dinner, you need only two other things: salty feta and caviar-like black lentils. The feta comes in handy twice. First, the milky brine deglazes and seasons the peppers as they sauté. (This works with just about any vegetable.) Second, meaty slabs take center stage where you might expect to see, well, meat. And the lentils do double duty, too. After getting simmered, some join forces with the peppers. The rest get olive oil–fried for a crunchy topping, not unlike potato chips, for everyone to scatter on top. If you live near a bakery, this is a nice time to swing by and pick up a crusty loaf or pillowy flatbread to tear by hand and use instead of a fork.

SERVES 4

Extra-virgin olive oil

6 bell peppers, stems and seeds removed, sliced into thick strips

Kosher salt

10 ounces (285g) feta, cut into 4 slabs, brine reserved

1 cup (240g) black lentils

Set the largest skillet you've got over medium heat and add 2 tablespoons oil. When that's hot, add the bell peppers, toss, then cover the skillet. Cook for 10 minutes to wilt, then season with ¼ teaspoon salt. Cook uncovered, stirring occasionally and lowering the heat as needed to prevent burning, until the peppers are soft and jammy, 25 to 35 minutes. Along the way, deglaze with a splash of feta brine whenever the peppers start to stick to the bottom (about ¼ cup/60ml in total).

While the peppers are working, cook the lentils. Combine 2 cups (480ml) water, the lentils, and ¼ teaspoon salt in a saucepan over medium-high heat and bring to a boil. Immediately drop the heat to its lowest setting and cover. Simmer for 20 to 35 minutes, until the lentils are tender with some bite, and drain.

Reserve ¾ cup (145g) of the cooked lentils and stir the rest into the peppers. Adjust the heat under the peppers to low and nestle in the feta. While that warms up, set a large cast-iron or nonstick skillet over medium heat and add enough oil to coat the bottom. When that's hot, add the ¾ cup reserved lentils and sprinkle with salt. Cook, tossing every so often, until the lentils are crispy and crackly, 5 to 10 minutes.

As soon as the feta is soft and warm, turn off the heat and drizzle some oil over the peppers and cheese. Serve with the crispy lentils on top.

how to peel an egg without destroying it

Along with chopping onions and making marinade by the gallon, one of my prep tasks as a line cook was peeling soft-boiled eggs. Here's how to avoid that caught-in-a-ceiling-fan look: Roll the shell around on a counter until it's cracked all over. Return the egg to the water and peel it while submerged—the bottom is usually the best place to start. The water will ease the shell right off, leaving behind an egg pristine enough for a restaurant service.

green beans with potatoes, olives & smashed eggs

Julia Child defined the French salade Niçoise as a "combination salad," a term we can all aspire to use more often. ("I made the best combination salad the other day." "What's in that combination salad you're eating?") As you'd expect, there's a lot going on: Anchovies, olives, tomatoes, potatoes, green beans, hard-boiled eggs, and lettuce—that's not even touching the vinaigrette—all support a centerpiece of canned tuna, which I love (and talk more about on page 98). But in this case, I don't think we need it. Because if you gave me a plate of crispy potatoes and jammy eggs, I'd be happy as a clam. And if you threw in some snappy green beans, crunchy-roasted olives, and an olive oil–olive brine dressing? Forget about it. And so this recipe stops right there.

Heat the oven to 450°F (230°C). Fill a stockpot with water and set over high heat to come to a boil.

Roughly chop the olives (if the pieces are too small, they'll burn) and place on a rimmed baking sheet along with the potatoes, 3 tablespoons oil, and ½ teaspoon salt. Toss until everything is coated, then evenly spread out. Roast the potatoes and olives for about 40 minutes, shuffling with a spatula halfway through.

Trim the woody ends of the green beans, then halve crosswise. When the water is boiling, generously season it with salt, then add the green beans. Cook for 2 to 4 minutes, until almost as tender as you'd like. (They'll continue to cook out of the water.) Use a spider or tongs to transfer the beans to a big bowl. (Don't drain the water or turn off the heat—we're using it again.) Dress the beans with 1 tablespoon oil and 1½ tablespoons olive brine. Taste and adjust both as needed. Add the potatoes and olives, and toss to combine.

Carefully lower the eggs into the boiling water and set a timer for 6½ minutes. When the eggs are done, transfer them to a bowl and fill with cold water and ice to shock. Peel (see tip opposite).

Transfer the green bean–potato mixture to a platter and top with the peeled eggs. Use a fork to break each egg into haphazard pieces. Drizzle with more oil and brine.

SERVES 4

1 cup (155g) pitted, drained Kalamata olives, brine reserved

2 pounds (910g) small potatoes, halved and/or quartered

Extra-virgin olive oil

Kosher salt

1½ pounds (685g) green beans

6 large eggs

socca with mushrooms & ricotta

Socca is hugely popular in Nice, and it's easy to see why. Besides being crackly-edged and gluten-free, socca comes together with one magical ingredient: chickpea, aka garbanzo bean, flour (mixed with water, salt, and sometimes oil). This crêpe-like flatbread made its way to France via Italy (where it's known as farinata), and is traditionally seen as a street snack—eaten out of hand, on the move. But I love to turn it into dinner with whatever's hanging around in the fridge. Once you try chile-jolted mushrooms (psst, more uses for harissa on page 102) and custardy ricotta, branch out to Brie and prosciutto, or roasted vegetables and Greek yogurt, or greens and eggs (like the puff pancake on page 80).

SERVES 3 TO 4

1 cup (115g) chickpea flour

Kosher salt

5 tablespoons (75ml) extra-virgin olive oil

1½ pounds (685g) mushrooms (such as baby bella, shiitake, or maitake), halved or quartered

1 tablespoon harissa, plus more to taste

1⅓ cups (320g) fresh ricotta

½ bunch flat-leaf parsley, leaves left whole, stems minced

Heat the oven to 450°F (230°C) and immediately stick a 12-inch (30cm) or 13-inch (33cm) cast-iron skillet inside.

Combine the chickpea flour and ¾ teaspoon salt in a medium bowl. Slowly stir in 1 cup (240ml) room-temp water (I do this by pouring a small splash, then mixing, over and over). The batter should be smooth and heavy cream-like in consistency. Stir in 1 tablespoon of the oil.

Place the mushrooms on a rimmed baking sheet, drizzle with 2 tablespoons of the oil, toss, and spread into an even layer. Roast until the mushrooms are deeply browned and crispy, about 35 minutes.

After the mushrooms have been in the oven for 25 minutes, carefully remove the hot skillet and set it on the stove over medium-high heat. Add the remaining 2 tablespoons of the oil and swirl to coat. Once the oil is hot, pour in the socca batter and tilt the pan to spread it out as much as possible. Turn off the stove and transfer the socca back to the oven for 10 minutes, until the top looks dry.

Remove the mushrooms and socca from the oven, turn on the broiler, and place a rack about 6 inches (15cm) from the heat. Slide the socca under the broiler and toast until the edges start to char and the top is golden brown, 2 to 4 minutes, checking often. Toss the roasted mushrooms with the harissa, then season with more harissa and salt to taste.

You can use a spatula to flip the socca onto a cutting board, slice it into wedges, divide these among plates, and top evenly with the ricotta, mushrooms, and parsley, plus a pinch of salt. Or just pile on the toppings right in the skillet and serve from there.

asparagus & cashews with green polenta

Polenta often earns its creaminess from butter or cheese or both. This vegan version needs neither. Instead, cashews and asparagus are blanched until soft, then whirled into a satiny puree you'll want to lap up by the bowlful. Don't. Swirl it into the warm polenta, which has a can't-put-your-finger-on-it cheesiness, courtesy of nutritional yeast. You could call this dinner and done—but, better to use all of these ingredients once more. Stir-fry asparagus and cashews until glowy and golden, then toss with more nutritional yeast because once you start, it's hard to stop. You'll see.

Combine the cornmeal, 1 teaspoon salt, and 5 cups (1.2L) water in a pot and set over medium-high heat to come to a boil, whisking often. When it starts to boil, drop the heat to low, cover the pot, and set a timer for 40 minutes. Every 5 minutes, whisk the polenta.

Meanwhile, set a pot with 4 cups (950ml) water over medium-high heat. Separate the asparagus into two groups: 1¼ pounds (570g) and 12 ounces (340g). Trim the woody ends. Chop the bigger group into 2-inch (5cm) pieces, and chop the smaller group into 1-inch (2.5cm) pieces.

When the water reaches a boil, generously season it with salt. Add the smaller group of asparagus plus ½ cup (70g) of the cashews. Cook for 5 minutes, until tender, then use a spider to transfer the asparagus and cashews to a blender. Add ¼ cup (60ml) of the blanching liquid. With the keyhole in the lid open and a towel pressed on top, blend until smooth. Season with salt to taste. Cover to keep warm.

Set your largest skillet over medium-high heat. Add 2 tablespoons of the oil. When it's hot, add the remaining asparagus and a couple pinches of salt. Cook, tossing as little as possible, until the asparagus is starting to char and is crisp-tender, about 4 minutes. Dump the asparagus onto a plate and lower the heat to medium-low. Add the remaining 1 tablespoon oil, the remaining 1 cup (140g) cashews, and a pinch of salt. Cook, tossing frequently, until the cashews are toasty, 5 to 7 minutes. Turn off the heat and return the asparagus to the skillet. Drizzle with oil, add 2 tablespoons of the nutritional yeast, and toss. Season with salt to taste.

When the polenta is done (smooth and thick, with no residual crunch), whisk in the remaining 2 tablespoons nutritional yeast and season with salt to taste. Divide the polenta among four bowls. Top evenly with the asparagus-cashew puree in polka dots, then use a spoon to swirl. Top each portion with the sautéed asparagus and cashews.

SERVES 4

1 cup (140g) coarse cornmeal

Kosher salt

2 pounds (910g) asparagus

1½ cups (210g) cashews

3 tablespoons extra-virgin olive oil

¼ cup (25g) nutritional yeast

sweet stuff to start
or end the day

apple-cheddar turnovers

Here's how to make pie dough in one sentence: Cut fat into flour, then add cold water until it holds together when squeezed, like you would a baby's cheek. The big question mark is the fat. You could go with butter for flavor, or shortening for flakiness, or a combo for flavorful flakiness. Or you could go with cheddar cheese. This ingredient is flavorful to the nines (think cheese straws, Cheez-Its, Goldfish, sunshine, rainbows) and all but guarantees tender dough with a crackly crust. It's a welcome update for apple—or pear or peach—turnovers, as ready for breakfast as they are for dessert. Now about those apples: Pick a variety that's sweet-tart in flavor and holds its own when baked. I like Pink Lady, Granny Smith, Jonagold, or Braeburn.

MAKES 4

all-cheddar pastry

1 cup plus
2 tablespoons (160g)
all-purpose flour,
plus more for rolling

1 teaspoon light
brown sugar

½ teaspoon kosher salt

5 ounces (140g) sharp
cheddar, grated

apple filling

1 pound (455g) apples,
peeled, cored, halved,
and sliced

¼ cup (50g) lightly
packed light
brown sugar

1½ tablespoons
all-purpose flour

½ teaspoon kosher salt

To make the pastry, combine the flour, sugar, and salt in a food processor and pulse. Add the cheddar and pulse a few more times to incorporate. Evenly pour 6 tablespoons (90ml) cold water on top, then pulse in short bursts until the mixture looks like cottage cheese and the sides of the food processor are no longer dusty, adding more water if needed. The dough should not turn into a big blob but should effortlessly hold together when squeezed. Dump onto a piece of plastic wrap, form into a square, and tightly seal. Chill for 45 minutes to 2 days.

When you're ready to bake, heat the oven to 375°F (190°C). (If you have a baking stone, great—place that in the oven.) Line a baking sheet with parchment or a silicone mat. Combine the apples, sugar, flour, and salt in a bowl and toss.

Remove the dough from the fridge and cut into four even pieces. Dust a clean work surface with flour. Roll each piece into a 6-inch (15cm) square.

Evenly divide the apple mixture among the dough squares. Close each pastry from corner to corner to form a triangle, stretching the dough as needed and pressing firmly so there's no air in the middle. If it tears along the way, just pull a little dough from the edge to patch it up. Crimp the edges of each turnover with a fork. Cut three slits in the top with a paring knife.

Transfer the turnovers to the baking sheet. Bake (with the baking sheet on the baking stone if you're using one) for 30 to 35 minutes, until the tops and bottoms are browned. Let cool for at least 20 minutes.

crunchy croissant brittle

While many brittles involve standing over the stove, boiling sugar, and using a candy thermometer, this recipe wants nothing to do with such fuss. Just warm half-and-half and sugar, soak croissant slices like French toast, and bake in the oven. This scrappy idea hails from Sea Wolf bakery in Seattle, where co-owners Jesse and Kit Schumann dreamed up brittle as a way to salvage day-old croissants. Inspired by them, this salty-sweet recipe can be made with bakery croissants, sure, but also softer supermarket ones—and they don't have to be stale either. The brittle keeps for more than a week in an airtight container, though I don't expect you to have it around that long. Plunk a piece in ice cream and use it as a makeshift spoon. Or serve a few alongside very strong coffee and call it breakfast.

Heat the oven to 325°F (165°C). Line two baking sheets with parchment or silicone mats.

Using a serrated knife, thinly slice the croissants lengthwise—as if you were making a sandwich—into ¼- to ½-inch (6mm to 1.3cm) pieces. You should be able to get three to four pieces from each.

Over low heat, heat the half-and-half until warm. Turn off the heat, add the sugar and salt, and stir until dissolved. Pour into a shallow bowl.

Dip one croissant piece in the syrup and flip to coat. Gently squish the soaked piece between your fingers to squeeze out some excess—it should still be saturated, just not dripping. Transfer to one of the baking sheets. Repeat with the remaining croissant pieces, trying to group the bigger pieces on one baking sheet and the smaller pieces on another. (You might have surplus liquid.) Sprinkle each piece with sugar.

Bake for 45 minutes to 1 hour, rotating the baking sheets halfway through. At the 45-minute mark, check in—the smaller pieces may be ready to come out. The brittle is done when it is golden brown all over, darker around the edges, and dry to the touch.

Cool on the baking sheet until it's no longer hot, then peel the parchment away from the brittle (not the other way around). Transfer to a cooling rack to cool completely. When the brittle cools, it should be completely crisp. (If it has cooled for 15 minutes and still feels softish, just continue to bake for another 5 minutes.)

**MAKES ABOUT
1 DOZEN PIECES**

4 croissants

1 cup (240ml)
half-and-half

1½ cups (300g)
granulated sugar, plus
more for sprinkling

1 teaspoon kosher salt

strawberry crumble with pretzel streusel

At its most basic, streusel has the same ingredients as shortbread—flour, sugar, butter, and salt—though you could add a bevy of bonuses like ground cinnamon or toasted nuts or cocoa powder. I'd rather substitute than add. When the list is so little to begin with, one swap makes a gargantuan difference. Try, for instance, ditching the all-purpose flour and pivoting to the snack aisle. Like the saltines on page 148, pretzels are a food processor–pulse away from becoming an overachieving flour—salty, savory, ready to conquer the world. They're a natural partner for spring strawberries, as the Southern dessert strawberry pretzel salad (not actually a salad) confirms. That said, this streusel is also good with non-strawberry crumbles, like apples in the fall and peaches in the summer. Serve with vanilla ice cream, crème fraîche, or a big pour of cream.

SERVES 6 TO 8

2 pounds (910g) strawberries, hulled, larger berries quartered, smaller ones halved

3 tablespoons plus ½ cup (135g) granulated sugar

5 ounces (140g) small pretzel twists (3⅔ cups)

⅛ teaspoon kosher salt

7 tablespoons (100g) unsalted butter, cubed, at a cool room temperature

Heat the oven to 375°F (190°C). Add the strawberries and 3 tablespoons sugar to a bowl and stir. Dump the pretzels into a food processor and blend until they're as fine as flour. Transfer 2 tablespoons of this pretzel flour to the bowl with the strawberries and stir again.

Add the remaining ½ cup (100g) sugar and the salt to the food processor and pulse a few times. Add the butter and process until it's totally incorporated, like shortbread dough, and the mixture just holds together when squeezed.

Transfer the strawberries to a 9-inch (23cm) cake or tart pan, at least 2 inches (5cm) in height. Top with the pretzel streusel, squeezing the mixture into clumps as you sprinkle it on top. Bake for 25 to 30 minutes, until the fruit juices are bubbling around the edges and look slightly thickened. Cool for at least 20 minutes before serving. This is best the day it's made.

whole-wheat cream scones

Like biscuits, scones should have a confident crust and fluffy center, be barely sweet and extremely buttery. But you don't need butter to get there. While classic scones involve stirring dry ingredients, cutting in butter, and binding with cream, cream scones increase the liquid and ignore the second step. And for good reason: Because there's no butter, there's no butter-incorporating. And because there's no butter-incorporating, there's no worrying about cutting it too small (dense scones), or leaving it too big (greasy scones), or letting it melt before they reach the oven (more dense scones). The cream takes care of everything.

Now about those other ingredients: White whole-wheat flour has more to say than all-purpose, but isn't as stodgy as standard whole-wheat. Likewise, Demerara sugar, versus granulated, brings butterscotchy vibes and a craggy-sparkly crust. On a perfect Sunday morning, I'm eating these, still in bed, with crème fraîche and apricot jam.

Heat the oven to 400°F (200°C). (If you have a baking stone, great—place that in the oven.)

Add the flour, sugar, baking powder, and salt to a large bowl and stir. Add about half of the cream, stir a few times, then add the rest in splashes, gently stirring until a mostly cohesive dough forms. Add more cream if needed; the dough should be sticky but not soupy.

Finish bringing the dough together by hand until there are no noticeable dry spots, then transfer it to a lightly floured work surface. Use your hands to pat the dough into a circle that's 6 inches (15cm) wide and 1 inch (2.5cm) high. Cut into six triangles. Brush the tops with cream, then sprinkle with Demerara, and don't skimp on either.

Transfer the scones to a parchment-lined baking sheet, spacing them out evenly. Bake (with the baking sheet on the baking stone if you're using one) for about 20 minutes, until bouncy to the touch, with browned bottoms and golden crusts.

These are best the day they're baked, especially when slightly warm. But no one will complain if you have leftovers: Wrap and freeze for up to 1 month, thaw at room temperature overnight, and refresh in a toaster.

MAKES 6

2 cups (240 grams) white whole-wheat flour, plus more for shaping

2 tablespoons Demerara sugar, plus more for sprinkling

3¼ teaspoons baking powder

1 teaspoon kosher salt

1¼ to 1½ cups (300 to 360ml) heavy cream, plus more for brushing

hazelnut cake with sour cream–chocolate frosting

I stumbled on this three-ingredient template—eggs, sugar, and nuts—thanks to cookbook author Emiko Davies, who shared a torta di noci (Calabrian walnut cake) on Food52 years back. I pivoted to ground hazelnuts, which act as a tender flour and flavorful fat. The result is dreamily dense and moist. And gluten-free. Because we're already using hazelnuts and sugar, it'd be wrong not to whip up a brittle with those same ingredients. I can't stress how worth it this is. Smash into glassy shards and glittery dust, then scatter on top like sprinkles. The frosting was inspired by our co-founder Amanda Hesser, whose family-famous dump-it cake is slathered in chocolatey sour cream. I like mine with dark chocolate, which pushes the whole cake in a less-sweet, more-sultry direction. Heads up: The baked cake has to chill out in the fridge for 8 to 24 hours to become its fudgiest, squidgiest, happiest self.

**MAKES ONE
9-INCH CAKE**

hazelnut cake

4 large eggs, at
room temperature

1 cup (200g)
granulated sugar

1 teaspoon kosher salt

12 ounces (340g)
raw hazelnuts

hazelnut brittle

3 ounces (85g) raw
hazelnuts, roughly
chopped

¾ cup (150g)
granulated sugar

Kosher or flaky salt

Heat the oven to 350°F (175°C). Grease a 9-inch (23cm) cake pan (with spray, butter, or oil), then line the bottom with parchment.

Separate the eggs, adding the yolks to a large bowl and the whites to a stand mixer fitted with the whisk attachment. Beat the whites, starting at low and gradually increasing the speed to medium-high, until stiff peaks form. Add the sugar and salt to the egg yolks and stir until pale yellow and thick.

Pulse the hazelnuts in a food processor until a sandy meal forms, but not so long that they turn into nut butter. Add the ground nuts to the egg yolk mixture and stir. Plop by plop, gently fold the whipped egg whites into the hazelnut mixture, taking care to deflate them as little as possible. Pour into the cake pan.

Bake for 28 to 32 minutes, until the cake is pillowy to the touch with golden-brown edges and a cake tester comes out clean.

To make the brittle, while the oven is still at 350°F (175°C), add the chopped hazelnuts to a parchment-lined baking sheet and roast until they're deeply toasted and fragrant, 6 to 10 minutes. Add the sugar to a small saucepan and pour 2 tablespoons water on top. Bring to a boil over medium-high heat and cook until it turns the color of maple syrup; you can gently swirl the pan toward the end to encourage even cooking but avoid stirring, which can cause crystallization. As soon as the sugar caramelizes, cut the heat and use a heatproof flexible spatula to stir in the warm hazelnuts. Scrape this mixture back onto the lined baking sheet, spreading it out as much as possible. (It hardens quickly.) Sprinkle with salt and cool completely before transferring to an airtight container, breaking into pieces if needed.

continued

sour cream–chocolate frosting

3½ ounces (100g) dark chocolate (67 to 72 percent cacao), chopped

1⅓ cups (320g) sour cream, at room temperature

Once the cake is totally cool, remove it from the pan. Wrap and refrigerate it for 8 to 24 hours. Remove the cake from the fridge an hour or so before frosting and serving if you want it at room temperature.

When you're ready to frost the cake, melt the chocolate in a double boiler or microwave, then let it cool until barely warm. Stir in a spoonful of sour cream until smooth, then repeat until you have about ⅓ cup (80g) left. Swirl the chocolate frosting on top of the cake, then randomly dollop on the remaining sour cream like polka dots. Use an offset spatula or spoon to swirl the frosting, so there are distinct swooshes of chocolate frosting and sour cream.

Add some brittle to a mortar and pestle and smash so some pieces are as fine as sprinkles and others still chunky (a cutting board and knife also works). Shower onto the cake. Odds are, you'll have some leftover brittle, which I've found is a very good thing.

minimalist frostings your desserts deserve

Just as frosting doesn't need to be overly sweet, it doesn't need to be overly complicated either. Put any of these two-ingredient recipes (add a pinch of salt, if you please) toward the flourless hazelnut cake on page 142—or any other single-layer cake that strikes your fancy.

goat cheese

10 ounces (285g) goat cheese

+

1 cup (120g) confectioners' sugar

↓

blend in food processor,
chill until cold

sweet potato

1 cooked large sweet potato
(skin removed)

+

½ cup (120ml) sweetened
condensed milk

↓

blend in food processor,
chill until cold

peanut butter

1 cup (240ml) heavy cream

+

½ cup (135g) creamy sweetened
peanut butter

↓

whisk to soft peaks,
use right away

apricot jam

8 ounces (225g) cream cheese

+

⅓ cup (105g) apricot jam

↓

blend in food processor,
use right away or chill for later,
with more jam on top

slightly less low maintenance

If you're feeling ambitious, you can add an extra step to give these cookies a roasty-toasty mood. After heating the oven, add the oats to a rimmed baking sheet and bake for about 12 minutes, until golden brown and nutty-fragrant, rotating the pan and tossing the oats halfway through. Let cool completely before moving on to step two. (You can use toasted oats just about anywhere you would use raw ones.)

low-maintenance oatmeal cookies

The internet cooks up all sorts of trends, like sweet potato toast (sweet potato you put in a toaster), cloud eggs (fluffed-up whites with a yolk belly button), ice cream bread (melted ice cream plus self-rising flour), and three-ingredient oatmeal cookies. (Yes, one of those is oats.) But the other two ingredients might surprise you: mashed banana and peanut butter. The catch is, if you add bananas to a cookie, it will taste like a banana cookie, and if you add peanut butter to a cookie, it will taste like a peanut butter cookie.

This recipe still has three ingredients, with a couple of swaps. To avoid a fruity flavor, we ditch the banana and return to a more classic sweetener: brown sugar. Its toffee vibes give these cookies tons of complexity without overshadowing the oats. And when it comes to fat, we'll call in something that's less in-your-face than peanut butter but still dairy-free: tahini. All you have to do is combine in a bowl—a splash of water encourages everyone to get along—then scoop and bake. If there was ever a cookie meant to be paired with coffee and called breakfast, this is it.

Heat the oven to 350°F (175°C). Line two baking sheets with parchment or silicone mats.

Add the oats, brown sugar, and salt to a bowl. Rub the mixture between your palms to break up any sugar lumps. Add the tahini and 2 tablespoons water and stir until a sticky dough forms. (If needed, you can add more water in ½-teaspoon increments until the dough comes together.)

Scoop the dough in heaping tablespoons onto the baking sheets. Use your palm to gently smush each blob into a disc about 2 inches (5cm) in diameter.

Bake for 12 to 14 minutes, until the edges just start to brown. The cookies will look almost underbaked, but they'll continue to crisp. Cool completely on a rack before eating. Store any leftovers in an airtight container for a few days or freeze for up to 1 month.

MAKES 16 COOKIES

1½ cups (150g)
rolled oats

¾ cup (150g) lightly
packed light
brown sugar

½ teaspoon kosher salt

⅔ cup (195g)
stirred tahini

lime posset with saltine streusel

I first caught wind of possets—custards made with thickened cream—thanks to Food52er MrsLarkin, who shared a puckery, lemony version on the site in 2010. Her recipe racked up almost 200 glowy reviews, such as: "Licked the pot clean." Or, "Tastes just like a Creamsicle!!!" While most custards rely on finicky thickening agents (egg yolks, cornstarch, or gelatin), possets turn to citrus juice. The acidity magically sets the cream while you get on with your day. To dial up the brightness even more, I throw in the zest too, so opt for organic fruit if possible. As for the crumbly-crunchy topping: Graham crackers are a great option (think: key lime pie). But even better are saltines, inspired by Bill Smith's Atlantic Beach Pie, another favorite on the site. The sunny contrast of citrus and salt is hard to beat.

SERVES 4

saltine streusel

2¼ ounces (60g) saltines (about 20 crackers)

2 tablespoons granulated sugar

¼ teaspoon kosher salt

3 tablespoons unsalted butter, melted

lime posset

2 cups (480ml) heavy cream

⅔ cup (130g) granulated sugar

2 teaspoons finely grated lime zest

Pinch of kosher salt

⅓ cup (80ml) freshly squeezed lime juice

Heat the oven to 350°F (175°C).

Add the saltines to a bowl and crush by hand until most are fine like cornmeal, with a few bigger pieces here and there. Stir in the sugar and salt, then the butter. Spread the mixture onto a parchment-lined rimmed baking sheet and bake for 10 to 15 minutes, tossing the streusel and rotating the pan halfway through, until golden brown and toasty.

To make the posset, combine the cream, sugar, lime zest, and salt in your largest saucepan (cream loves boiling over and no one loves cleaning that up) over medium-high heat. Bring to a boil and cook for 5 minutes. Turn off the heat and whisk in the lime juice. Let cool off the heat for 15 minutes to thicken slightly.

Find four vessels for the possets (dessert coupes, water glasses, or custard ramekins all work). If you're eating within a day, layer some streusel at the bottom of each glass (estimate 2 tablespoons per serving). Otherwise, serve all of the streusel as a topping.

Slowly pour the posset into your vessels. Cover and chill until firm and set, 3 to 5 hours.

Serve cold with the streusel sprinkled on top.

balsamic posset with berries

Sure, you can swap out the lime for other citrus juices, like lemon or grapefruit. But you can also branch out to tangy balsamic vinegar. Just omit the lime zest and juice, and swap in 3 tablespoons (45ml) balsamic vinegar. Once chilled, the top should be thick and the bottom slightly custardier. Instead of streusel on top, couple up with fresh berries (sugared, or not)—strawberries are peak.

so long, fuzz

Along with a dry sense of humor, I inherited an unexplainable aversion to peach fuzz from my grandmother. The mention alone has us covered in goose bumps. But we still love peaches! If you're in a similar boat, here's a work-around: Bring a pot of water to a boil. Set up an ice bath. Use a serrated knife to cut an X on the tushie of each peach. Lower as many as will fit into the boiling water and cook for 30 seconds to 1 minute, until the X starts to fray. Transfer to the ice bath and peel—the skin should slip right off.

buttermilk granita with black-peppered peaches

At its laziest, ice cream involves stirring together a few ingredients and churning them in an ice cream machine. But, you know, you still need an ice cream machine. In this recipe, you don't. Because we aren't making ice cream—we're making ice cream's scrappy, handsome, funny (and single!) Italian cousin, granita. This is as foolproof as frozen dessert gets, with no special equipment needed. Though it often starts with a lean liquid, like juice or coffee, this granita turns to tangy buttermilk. Think: the tart flavor of frozen yogurt and flaky texture of shaved ice. And all atop a puddle of syrupy peaches. It goes without saying that you can swap out the peaches for nectarines, plums, or apricots. Just don't skip the black pepper—it gets along with fruit even better than cinnamon.

Combine the buttermilk, ⅓ cup (65g) of the sugar, and ¼ teaspoon salt in an 8-inch (20cm) square baking dish. Stir until the sugar dissolves. Freeze for 45 to 60 minutes, until the perimeter starts to harden. Remove from the freezer and use a fork to scrape the frozen edges toward the center and shuffle everything around. Freeze for another 30 minutes, then scrape and shuffle with the fork again. Repeat this—mixing every 30 minutes—until the granita is totally frozen and snowy in texture. (This will take 2 to 3 hours total.) At this point, you can eat right away or transfer to an airtight container and store in the freezer for up to 2 weeks.

When you want to eat, combine the sliced peaches, the remaining 2 tablespoons sugar, and a pinch each of salt and pepper in a bowl. Taste and adjust the seasoning depending on the fruit's sweetness. Let this hang out, at room temperature or in the fridge, until the fruit is super syrupy, 15 to 30 minutes. Taste and adjust the seasoning again if needed.

To serve, divide the fruit among four bowls, glasses, or dessert coupes, making sure to get all those good juices in there, too. Top each with a mound of granita and eat ASAP, preferably outside.

SERVES 4

2 cups (480ml) buttermilk

⅓ cup plus 2 tablespoons (90g) granulated sugar

Kosher salt

4 ripe peaches, sliced into thin wedges

Freshly ground black pepper

a frozen banana is instant soft-serve

The next time you have a banana that is halfway to mush, don't throw it out, but don't make banana bread either. Try this secretly vegan ice cream instead. I learned this technique from Faith Durand and The Kitchn, via Food52's Genius Recipes column. Our founding editor, Kristen Miglore, broke down the magic-slash-science as such: "As the blades slice through the frozen banana, pectin chains form and the banana churns up into the spitting image of soft-serve ice cream, with the most intense banana flavor this side of Chunky Monkey." And who doesn't want that? These days, I make it as often for breakfast as I do for dessert. Sometimes I stick to the one-ingredient classic. Often I add a wildcard ingredient, or three. Don't worry about measurements. Just follow this basic route—the detours along the way are up to you.

1.

Peel a very ripe banana. (Or, if your bananas are small, scale up to 1½ or 2 bananas per portion.) Break the fruit into pieces, pop them in a baggie (bonus points if it's reusable), and throw it in the freezer.

2.

As soon as the fruit is firm—or the next day or week or month—stick a serving dish in the freezer. Transfer the frozen banana to a food processor (if the pieces have fused together, roughly chop them first). Pulse until crumbly.

3.

Toss in up to two mix-ins (see page opposite). Keep blending, scraping down the sides as needed, until the mixture is almost as floofy and creamy as soft-serve. Which, now that you mention it, is what you just made.

4.

Scrape the mixture into the frozen dish and grab a spoon. Or sprinkle or drizzle up to two toppings (see page opposite).

mix-ins

buttermilk or kefir

heavy cream, half-and-half,
or whole milk

oat milk or another
nondairy fave

cocoa powder or
malted milk powder

instant espresso or matcha

white miso

frozen berries

crème fraîche, greek
yogurt, or sour cream

peanut butter, almond
butter, tahini, nutella, etc.

toppings

melted chocolate,
especially dark

halvah

toasted nuts

hazelnut brittle (page 142)

honey, maple syrup, or
pomegranate molasses

whipped cream

peanut butter cups

spoonable jam

extra-virgin olive oil

oatmeal cookies (page 147)

highly recommended combos

cashew butter
+
melted chocolate

———————

frozen cherries
+
halvah

———————

cocoa powder
+
extra-virgin olive oil

———————

oat milk
+
salted peanuts

———————

instant espresso
+
whipped cream

flourless walnut brownies

Flour is the difference between a fudgy brownie and a cakey brownie—the more you add, the cakier it gets. So what would happen if you didn't add any flour? And what is flour, anyway? While the default used to be all-purpose flour, nowadays there is a truckload of non-wheat ingredients calling themselves flour, from nuts (like almonds) to grains (like oats) to legumes (like chickpeas). These come in handy if you have a wheat allergy or intolerance—or if you want a super-fudgy brownie.

In this Passover-ready dessert, we'll take advantage of an ingredient that most brownie recipes already include: walnuts. Some get toasted and stirred into the batter. Others are left raw, for a wheat-ish subtleness, and whooshed in a food processor. The rest of the recipe is as classic as it gets, inspired by Alice Medrich's cocoa brownies to end all cocoa brownies. Thanks to the walnuts' buttery fat and zero gluten, the result is rich, crackly, and halfway to chocolate ganache.

MAKES ONE 8-INCH (20CM) SQUARE PAN

⅔ cup plus ¾ cup (170g) chopped walnuts

½ cup (115g) unsalted butter

1 cup (80g) cocoa powder

1¼ cups (250g) granulated sugar

¼ teaspoon kosher salt

2 large eggs

Heat the oven to 350°F (175°C). Line an 8-inch (20cm) square baking dish with parchment, with overhang on two sides to lift out the baked brownies.

Place ⅔ cup (80g) of the walnuts on a baking sheet and toast in the oven for 7 to 10 minutes, until fragrant and golden brown.

While those cool, add the remaining ¾ cup (90g) walnuts to a food processor and pulse in short bursts until a crumbly meal forms. (Don't take it too far, or you'll end up with walnut butter.)

Add the butter to a medium saucepan and set over low heat. When that's melted, remove from the heat and use a wooden spoon to stir in the cocoa powder, then the sugar and salt. Add the eggs, one at a time, stirring after each addition until incorporated. Set a timer and mix for 2 minutes (with feeling!), until the batter is smooth and glossy. Stir in the walnut flour, then the toasted walnuts.

Bake for about 25 minutes, until puffed around the edges with a glossy-crackly top and a toothpick inserted near a corner comes out mostly clean. Let cool until room temperature, then remove from the pan and cut into squares.

lemon bars with olive oil shortbread

When I was little, I used to ask for lemon bars as a birthday present (go figure), but it wasn't until years later that I realized how easy they are to make myself. This classic dessert already has a small ingredient list—flour, sugar, eggs, lemons, butter—because most of them are used twice, in both the crumbly shortbread and puckery curd. So there isn't room for trimming—but substituting? That we can do. Here, we'll ditch the butter and usher in grassy olive oil. This yields a crisp-tender, sorta-savory crust and softens the sharpness of the curd. Make sure to zest, then juice the lemons. You can cut 16 standard squares or 32 tiny ones. Leave them naked or shake on confectioners' sugar or maybe a pinch of flaky salt. Just serve them cold as can be; no forks allowed.

Heat the oven to 325°F (165°C). Line an 8-inch (20cm) square baking dish with parchment, with overhang on two sides to lift out the baked bars.

To make the shortbread, combine the flour, sugar, and salt in a bowl and stir. Add the oil and mix until a lumpy dough forms—don't overmix. Dump the dough into the pan, pat flat with your hand, and prick all over with a fork. Bake for 45 to 55 minutes, rotating halfway through, until puffed and golden brown.

While that bakes, mix up the lemon curd. Combine the sugar, lemon juice, eggs, flour, oil, zest, and salt in a bowl and whisk until smooth.

When the crust timer goes off, re-whisk the lemon mixture. Use oven mitts to pull out the oven rack. Carefully pour the lemon mixture onto the hot crust, then push the rack back and close the oven.

Bake for 25 to 35 minutes, rotating the pan halfway through, until the edges are puffy and the center barely jiggles when you nudge the pan.

Cool on a rack until room temperature, then cover and refrigerate until cold. Remove from the pan and cut into squares.

MAKES ONE 8-INCH (20CM) SQUARE PAN

olive oil shortbread

2 cups (280g) all-purpose flour

⅓ cup (65g) granulated sugar

½ teaspoon kosher salt

⅔ cup (160ml) extra-virgin olive oil

lemon curd

1¾ cups (350g) granulated sugar

1 cup (240ml) freshly squeezed lemon juice

6 large eggs

7 tablespoons (60g) all-purpose flour

2 tablespoons extra-virgin olive oil

1 tablespoon finely grated lemon zest

½ teaspoon kosher salt

acknowledgments

Where do I even begin? This book wouldn't be a twinkle in my eye without so many people.

Thank you to my family, especially my sweet parents, whose kitchen I destroyed for the first two decades of my life. My brother, Jake, for your advice and cat-texts. My sisters Bonnie, Liza, and Andrea, because I really believe that. My Aunt Margie, who I want to be when I grow up. My Grandma Jolly, for your resilience and paprika potatoes.

Thank you to literally everyone at Food52, with an extra high-five to our fearless director of content, Brinda Ayer, who encouraged me to write this book in the first place. I'm in awe of your guidance and wisdom and desk snacks. You're just the best.

Thank you to our cofounders, Amanda Hesser and Merrill Stubbs, and founding editor, Kristen Miglore, all of whom I looked up to long before I joined the team—when I needed inspiration to write, I read and reread cookbooks by the three of you.

Thank you to our SVP of content, Stacey Rivera, who teaches me at least seven things every time we chat. Ali Slagle, for your whip-smart edits and erasable pen. Kelsey Burrow, for your PR prowess and rallying. Suzanne D'Amato, for believing in me to launch this column (and coming up with its name!). And Joanna Sciarrino, for being the greatest mentor.

Thank you to the creative dream team: Our creative director, Alexis Anthony, who makes Food52 the most beautiful place, without whom this book wouldn't be possible. Our photographer, James Ransom, whose pictures (just look at them!) I want to frame. Our test kitchen director, Allison Buford, who can juggle a dozen recipes without blinking

an eye. Our senior food stylist, Anna Billingskog, who makes every ingredient feel seen. Our associate art director, Amanda Widis, and prop stylist, Brooke Deonarine, whose scenes I would like to live in. And our creative operations manager, Eddie Barrera, who makes all of it possible.

Thank you to everyone I crossed paths with in North Carolina, especially the Scratch crew, who taught me about so much more than just pie, and all the editors who took a chance on me. And the adoption center that led me to my cat, Butter!

Thank you to our illustrator, Hyesu Lee. Your beaming art, bright ideas, and endless positivity add so much joy to this book. I hope there are more projects in our future (or at least that I can turn one of your illos into a tattoo).

Thank you to Ten Speed Press for believing in a first-time author—to Julie Bennett, Emma Rudolph, Emma Campion, Lizzie Allen, Mari Gill, Serena Sigona, Monica Stanton, Kristin Casemore, and Windy Dorresteyn. I'm so grateful for your expert editing, knockout design, and years of collaboration. I've learned a thousand things from your team and this opportunity, to work for a publisher who has produced so many of my favorite cookbooks, still feels surreal.

Thank you, thank you, thank you to everyone who tested a recipe for this manuscript: Alisa Deitz, Amy and Scott Laperruque, Anna Gass, Andrea and CJ Quackenbush, Ashley and Rich Coleman, Bonnie Wertheim and EJ Harrison, Brinda Ayer and Danny Cumming, Brittany Johnson and Anthony Matthews, Carol and John Graham, Caroline Sequin and Ben (and Elisa) Acker, Claudia Rocha and Emerson Murphy-Hill, Colleen Brady, Denae and Ryan Robinson,

Elise Thomasset, Emily Kulesza, Emma Strickler, Emma Wilkinson and Jason Driscoll, Erin Alexander, Heather Krieger, Jake Laperruque, Jessica and Jared (and Layla and Makenna) Graham, Jessica Siegel, Joanna Sciarrino and Evan Cinq-Mars, Jolly Raiss, Kari Gutzmer Acker, Kate Knapp, Katie and Josh Donnelly, Katie Stolee, Kina Viola and Marty Cain, Kristen Miglore, Laura Becker, Leah Broadwell, Linda Silverman, Liza Seiden and Simon Paulenoff, Luke Smith, Mackenzie Walker, Mandy Genovese, Margie Philo, Meghan Doherty, Melissa Roth, Miriam Pinski and Julian Aronowitz, Nancy and Mark Smith, Patrick and Margaret Wilson, Rebecca Firkser, Stephanie Bourgeois, Susan Streit Sherman, Tara Huggins and Victoria Lin!

And last but the opposite of least, thank you to my husband, Justin. This is the only paragraph of the book you haven't read, and I've tried to write it a hundred times! All of the words fall flat in comparison to your support, humor, and warmth. The best thing that ever happened to me was meeting you.

index

Published in the United States by Ten Speed Press, an imprint of Random
House, a division of Penguin Random House LLC, New York.
www.tenspeed.com

Ten Speed Press and the Ten Speed Press colophon are registered trademarks
of Penguin Random House LLC.

Some of the material in this work first appeared on the Food52 website.

Library of Congress Cataloging-in-Publication Data
Names: Laperruque, Emma, 1992- author. | Ransom, James (Photographer),
    photographer.
Title: Food52 big little recipes : good food with minimal ingredients and
    maximal flavor / Emma Laperruque ; photographs by James Ransom.
Other titles: Food 52 big little recipes
Description: First edition. | California : Ten Speed Press, [2021] | Includes index.
Identifiers: LCCN 2020045750 (print) | LCCN 2020045751 (ebook) |
    ISBN 9780399581588 (hardcover) | ISBN 9780399581595 (ebook)
Subjects: LCSH: Quick and easy cooking. | LCGFT: Cookbooks.
Classification: LCC TX833.5 .L358 2021 (print) | LCC TX833.5 (ebook) |
    DDC 641.5/12—dc23
LC record available at https://lccn.loc.gov/2020045750
LC ebook record available at https://lccn.loc.gov/2020045751

Hardcover ISBN: 978-0-399-58158-8
eBook ISBN: 978-0-399-58159-5

Printed in China

Editor: Julie Bennett | Production editor: Emma Rudolph
Designer: Lizzie Allen | Art director: Emma Campion
Production designers: Mari Gill & Faith Hague
Production manager: Serena Sigona
Prepress color manager: Neil Spitkovsky
Creative director: Alexis Anthony
Food stylist: Anna Billingskog
Kitchen director: Allison Buford
Prop stylists: Amanda Widis & Brooke Deonarine
Copyeditor: Amy Kovalski | Proofreader: Amy Bauman
Indexer: Ken DellaPenta
Publicist: Kristin Casemore | Marketer: Monica Stanton

10 9 8 7 6 5 4 3 2 1

First Edition